WARRIOR • 144

ITALIAN BLACKSHIRT 1935–45

P CROCIANI & P P BATTISTELLI　　ILLUSTRATED BY G RAVA

Series editors Marcus Cowper and Nikolai Bogdanovic

First published in 2010 by Osprey Publishing
Midland House, West Way, Botley, Oxford OX2 0PH, UK
44–02 23rd St, Suite 219, Long Island City, NY 11101, USA
E-mail: info@ospreypublishing.com

ISBN: 978 184603 505 0
E-book ISBN: 978 1 84908 253 2

Editorial by Ilios Publishing, Oxford, UK (www.iliospublishing.com)
Design PDQ Media
Index by Fineline Editorial Services
Originated by PDQ Media

10 11 12 13   10 9 8 7 6 5 4 3 2 1

A CIP catalogue record for this book is available from the British Library.

ACKNOWLEDGEMENTS

The authors would like to thank the following people for their help: the
Archivio Ufficio Storico Stato Maggiore Esercito, the Archivio Centrale dello
Stato, the Istituto Nazionale per la Storia del Movimento di Liberazione in
Italia, the Laboratorio Storico-Iconografico della Facoltà di Scienze Politiche
Università di Roma Tre, Stefano Ales, Nikolai Bogdanovic, Prof. Giuseppe
Conti, Marcus Cowper, Dottor Luigi Gatti, Prof. Luigi Goglia, Dottor Andrea
Molinari, Bruno Nunziati, Christopher Pannell, Angelo L. Pirocchi, and Count
Ernesto G. Vitetti.

Readers are invited to note that the authors have chosen not to provide
details of the Blackshirts' involvement in Spain, given the particular
circumstances of their involvement there.

AUTHORS' NOTE

The Blackshirt divisions (save for in the Spanish Civil War) were named
after the anniversaries of the Fascist revolution. These included '23 Marzo'
(23 March 1919), '28 Ottobre' (28 October 1922), '3 Gennaio' (3 January
1925), '18 Febbraio' (1 February 1923) and '21 Aprile' (21 April). The latter
is the anniversary of the foundation of Rome, which in 1923 replaced
1 May as a national holiday.

ARTIST'S NOTE

Readers may care to note that the original paintings from which the
colour plates in this book were prepared are available for private sale.
All reproduction copyright whatsoever is retained by the Publishers.
All enquiries should be addressed to Giuseppe Rava via the following
website:

www.g-rava.it

The Publishers regret that they can enter into no correspondence upon
this matter.

THE WOODLAND TRUST

Osprey Publishing are supporting the Woodland Trust, the UK's leading
woodland conservation charity, by funding the dedication of trees.

FOR A CATALOGUE OF ALL BOOKS PUBLISHED BY OSPREY MILITARY
AND AVIATION PLEASE CONTACT:

Osprey Direct, c/o Random House Distribution Center,
400 Hahn Road, Westminster, MD 21157
Email: uscustomerservice@ospreypublishing.com

Osprey Direct, The Book Service Ltd, Distribution Centre,
Colchester Road, Frating Green, Colchester, Essex, CO7 7DW
E-mail: customerservice@ospreypublishing.com

www.ospreypublishing.com

CONTENTS

ITALIAN BLACKSHIRT 1935–45

INTRODUCTION

The origins of the *Camicie Nere* (Blackshirts) date back to the months after the end of World War I, when Italy was riven by social and political struggle. The *Squadre d'Azione* (action squads, their members being called *Squadristi*) came into being in reaction both to the 'mutilated victory' which deprived Italy of what she considered her rightful gains, and to the rise of the socialist-communist party. Controlled by Benito Mussolini, the *Squadre* were made up of war veterans and young people led by charismatic local fascist leaders known as *ras* (ringleaders), after the Ethiopian term for 'chief'; violence was the main instrument used to intimidate their adversaries, which led to frequent bouts of street-fighting. Their paramilitary organization had its roots both in the *Arditi*, the Italian assault units of World War I (see Warrior 87: *Italian Arditi*, Angelo L. Pirocchi, Osprey Publishing: Oxford, 2004), and in the legions of ancient Rome. The creation on 23 March 1919 of the Fasci di Combattimento (Fighting Fascists) gave a political basis to the movement, which was later transformed into the Partito Nazionale Fascista (National Fascist Party). The latter played a vital role in Mussolini's rise to power on 28 October 1922, when four columns of Blackshirts marched unopposed on Rome.

Mussolini, dressed in the uniform of Primo Caporale d'onore della Milizia, reviews a Blackshirt battalion, who are saluting with raised daggers in front of the MVSN's headquarters. To the right is Luogotenente Generale Enzo Galbiati, chief of staff of the MVSN from May 1941 to July 1943. (Archivio Centrale dello Stato, Rome)

Soon after this event, the Blackshirts' somewhat haphazard organization was incorporated within the framework of the nascent Fascist state. On 1 February 1923 the Milizia Volontaria Sicurezza Nazionale (MVSN, National Security Volunteer Militia) was officially created out of the Blackshirt cadre, both the rank and file and its leadership. This provided a twofold solution to a particular problem: firstly it brought an otherwise wildly irregular force that was often exclusively in the hands of the *ras* under control, and secondly it turned the Fascist Party's militia into a national institution. The MVSN was a nationwide organization with a territorial basis, like a territorial army, with almost every Italian province (equivalent to a county) or large city having its own *legione* (legion) that was itself subdivided into *coorti* (cohorts) and *centurie* (centuries), adopting the nomenclature of the ancient Roman army. The actual organization only provided a framework of service, as the Blackshirts were only called to duty when circumstances demanded.

The first duty of the MVSN was to maintain law and order. This also included conflict with any form of opposition to Mussolini and the Fascist regime, though this was now done via cooperating with the local state authorities and the police forces, rather than directly fighting them, as had been the case before Mussolini's rise to power. By the late 1920s the MVSN had changed from being a party militia into a state organization, and despite it growing ever larger in size it had by then lost most of its original ideological coherence. Policing duties were mainly taken back by the state police forces, which were now fully controlled by the Fascist authorities; only limited and highly specialized police tasks were retained by the special branches of the MVSN. Deprived of a great deal of their original political ethos, which survived mainly in their external appearance, the Blackshirts seemed destined merely to provide a decorative element to Fascist mass meetings and celebrations. However, it was precisely at this point that Mussolini created a new role for the Blackshirts, and they began to develop as a combat force.

CHRONOLOGY

1919	Mussolini organizes the *Squadre d'Azione* (Action Squads) to combat his political adversaries.
23 March 1919	Mussolini founds the Fasci di combattimento (Fighting Fascists) in Milan.
7 November 1921	The Fasci di combattimento are transformed into the Partito Nazionale Fascista (Fascist National Party). The *Squadre d'Azione* are brought under central control and reorganized; their members become known as *Camicie Nere* after their black shirts.
28 October 1922	Fascist 'march on Rome' takes place, leading to Mussolini's rise to power.
15 December 1922	The Fascist Grand Council creates the Milizia Volontaria Sicurezza Nazionale (MVSN).
1 February 1923	The *Squadre d'Azione* are disbanded and the Blackshirts are absorbed into it. Blackshirts legions are created throughout Italy.
1 September 1923	The first three combat legions are mobilized and sent to Libya.

13–17 June 1924	Following the murder of the Socialist member of parliament Giacomo Matteotti, Mussolini uses four combat legions to restore public order – the last time the Blackshirts will be used for civil-order duties.
1 August 1924	The MVSN is reorganized as part of the Italian armed forces, and swear loyalty to the king.
3 January 1925	Mussolini claims political responsibility for the killing of Matteotti, marking the beginning of his dictatorship.
9 October 1926	Mussolini becomes *Comandante Generale* (commander in chief) of the MVSN
November 1927	The Milizia per la difesa antiaerea del territorio (MDAT, anti-aircraft home defence) is created.
10 July 1928	The army frees up any Blackshirts aged between 26 and 36 to join the Blackshirt combat battalions; two battalions take part in army manoeuvres and later form Blackshirt legions.
29 March 1930	The legions are attached to Italian army divisions.
1934	The Milizia artiglieria da costa (DACOS, coastal artillery militia) is created.
5 December 1934	Border incidents occur between Italy and Ethiopia in Italian Somaliland.
Summer 1935	29 Blackshirt *legioni* or battalion groups are mobilized; these form seven divisions, five of which are deployed in Eritrea (plus one in Italian Somaliland). By October, there are 132 Blackshirt legions, each having one operational and one territorial battalion.
3 October 1935	Italy invades Ethiopia. After an early advance, operations stall, and in December General Badoglio takes over command.
January 1936	Italian forces resume the offensive, leading to the seizure of Addis Ababa in May 1936.
9 May 1936	Mussolini declares the birth of the 'new Roman empire'; shortly after the end of the Italo-Ethiopian War, the Blackshirt divisions are disbanded and the legions demobilized.
19 July 1936	The day after the outbreak of the Spanish Civil War, Francisco Franco asks for German and Italian support for the Nationalist cause; volunteer recruitment begins in Italy.
24 October 1936	The Rome–Berlin Axis, a German–Italian agreement, is founded.
18 November 1936	Mussolini decides to send an expeditionary corps to Spain.
22 December 1936	The first 3,000 Blackshirts (organized in *banderas* of battalion strength) arrive in Spain.
February 1937	After the battle of Malaga, three Blackshirt divisions are formed (1ª 'Dio lo vuole', 2ª 'Fiamme Nere', and 3ª 'Penne Nere').
18 March 1937	The 1ª 'Dio lo vuole' division is disbanded after the battle of Guadalajara.
November 1937	The remaining two Blackshirt divisions are merged into a single Blackshirt division, which is later disbanded in October 1938. The Blackshirt *banderas* are grouped into

	three mixed Italian–Spanish brigades ('Frecce Nere', 'Frecce Azzurre', and 'Frecce Verdi').
7 November 1938	The anti-aircraft and coastal artillery militias are transformed into the Milizia Artiglieria Contraerea (MACA) and Milizia Artiglieria Marittima (MILMART).
26 January 1939	The Blackshirts parade through Barcelona following Franco's victory in Catalonia.
6 April 1939	Italy invades Albania.
6 May 1939	Germany and Italy sign the Patto d'Acciaio (Pact of Steel) military alliance.
1 September 1939	Germany invades Poland. Mussolini declares Italy a 'non belligerent'.
18 September 1939	The Milizia Fascista Albanese (Albanian Fascist Militia) is formed in Albania. Four Blackshirt divisions are organized and sent to Libya.
May 1940	The third Blackshirt division in Libya is disbanded and used to reinforce the other three.
10 June 1940	Italy declares war on France and Great Britain.
20 June 1940	The first Blackshirt battalions to be mobilized take part in the Italian attack across the Western Alps. Four days later an armistice is agreed, leading to France's surrender.
3 August 1940	British Somaliland is attacked and overrun by Italian forces.
13 September 1940	The Italian advance to Sidi Barrani is spearheaded by the Blackshirt divisions; the advance is halted one week later.
28 October 1940	Italy attacks Greece from Albania, the advance is halted two weeks later.
29 October 1940	The legions are reorganized and full mobilization of the Blackshirt units begins. The office of 'Blackshirt inspector' is formed within the army staff, and many Blackshirt legions are sent to Albania.
14 November 1940	The Greek counterattack begins, pushing the Italians back to Albania by early December.
8 December 1940	The British Western Desert Force attacks the Italian positions at Sidi Barrani; the Blackshirt divisions retreat to Sollum and Bardia, where they are destroyed in January.
19 January 1941	British and Commonwealth forces attack Eritrea; the offensive against Italian East Africa starts in February.
6 April 1941	Germany attacks Greece, which surrenders on the 21st, and Yugoslavia is attacked by Germany, Italy and Hungary. Yugoslavia surrenders on the 18th, and Italy annexes Slovenia, Dalmatia and Montenegro, and occupies large portions of the country.
19 May 1941	The HQ of the Italian defence force in East Africa surrenders at Amba Alagi.
22 June 1941	Germany invades the Soviet Union. Mussolini sends an Italian expeditionary corps and a Blackshirt legion to Russia.
1 October 1941	The 'M' battalions are officially created.
Spring 1942	Mussolini sends an entire army to the Eastern Front along with two Blackshirt *raggruppamenti*; these units are badly mauled during the retreat following the Soviet winter offensive.

8 November 1942	The Allies land in French North Africa.
13 May 1943	Axis forces in North Africa surrender.
25 June 1943	The first 'M' armoured division is formed near Rome as Mussolini's bodyguard.
10 July 1943	The Allies land in Sicily.
25/26 July 1943	Mussolini is dismissed by the king and arrested; only one Blackshirt battalion near Rome tries to react to this, but soon fails.
8 September 1943	Italy surrenders, as Allied forces land at Salerno. German forces take over most of the country, and several Blackshirt units join them.
12 September 1943	Mussolini is rescued from captivity and taken to Germany.
18 September 1943	Mussolini announces the birth of the Repubblica Sociale Italiana (RSI).
6 December 1943	Following a reorganization of the armed forces, the royal government in southern Italy disbands the MVSN.
8 December 1943	In northern Italy, the Guardia Nazionale Repubblicana (GNR) is formed by absorbing the MVSN and the Carabinieri. Most Blackshirt units continue to fight under German command. Civil war rages throughout Italy.
21 June 1944	Mussolini transforms the Partito Fascista Repubblicano into a military organization following the creation of the Corpo Ausiliario delle Squadre d'Azione delle Camicie Nere modelled on the early Action Squads.
28 April 1945	Having attempted to escape to Switzerland, Mussolini is captured by partisans and executed; four days later German forces in Italy surrender.

ORGANIZATION AND DEVELOPMENT

The early years

The first Blackshirt units to be formed were the three battalion-sized *legioni* (legions – the 132ª, 171ª and 176ª) raised in 1923. These 2,900-strong units were sent to Libya to fight the local rebellion until demobilization in May 1924, when they were replaced by two standing *legioni* ('Oea' and 'Berenice'). Two other battalion-sized *legioni* were also mobilized in 1928 to take part in field exercises in northern Italy, after the army had made Blackshirts aged 26–36 available for this. On 1 September 1929 the military role of the Blackshirts was sanctioned by a change in the structure of the MVSN; up to 72 (though the actual number varied) Blackshirt battalions were now to be attached to army infantry divisions, as decreed on 29 March 1930 by the Fascist Grand Council, in a fixed ratio of two battalions per army division. However, as a consequence of both the army's opposition to this and a general reluctance by the Fascists to losing men, by July 1933 there were only 30 Blackshirt battalions comprising 20,000 men.

The real boost to the growth of the Blackshirts as a military force was given by Mussolini's decision to start a war against Ethiopia in 1935; he wanted them to spearhead the fighting. Between 1935 and 1936 seven Blackshirt divisions were formed, including 27 *legioni* and two *gruppi battaglioni* (battalion groups, equivalent to brigades) with a total strength in the 62

Milizia Volontaria Sicurezza Nazionale (MVSN)

The all-volunteer Milizia Volontaria Sicurezza Nazionale is unique in modern Italian military history, being matched only by pre-unification forces such as Garibaldi's Redshirts. It contended with the army, which was almost exclusively cadred via conscription. Enlistment in the MVSN was open to those in the 17–50 age group who were physically fit, not serving in the armed forces, and were members of the Partito Nazionale Fascista. They would be called to duty following the mobilization of their respective *legione* which, after 1925, mainly took place during Fascist mass meetings and festivities. The MVSN's strength grew from *c.* 277,000 in January 1928 to *c.* 399,000 in December 1931, though it dropped to 312,000 by June 1940. Having lost its political security role, the MVSN evolved both as a special police and as a military force. Besides combat units, from 1923 to 1928 the *milizie speciali* (special militias) were created, including the railway Milizia Ferroviaria, the port Milizia Portuaria, the post and telegraph Milizia Postelegrafica, the forestry Milizia Forestale, and the highway Milizia della Strada, followed by the Milizia per la difesa antiaerea del territorio (MDAT, later DICAT, anti-aircraft home defence) and the Milizia artiglieria da costa (DACOS, later MILMART, coastal defence). In 1939–40 the latter had a strength of 78,000 and 33,000 respectively, while the *milizie speciali* doubled in size from their 1930 strength to 48,000. This brought several changes to the MVSN's structure; those Blackshirts that resisted discipline, including several *Squadristi*, were soon replaced by the large number of youngsters who had joined the party after Mussolini's rise to power. Also, instead of pledging their allegiance to the service of 'God and the Italian Homeland' and being under direct orders from Mussolini, from 1 August 1924 the incorporation of the MVSN into the armed forces meant the Blackshirts now pledged allegiance to the king. These developments also meant that regular, territorial legions mainly worked as recruitment centres and depots; their numbers varied from 126 in 1926 to 135 in 1928, before falling to 120 in 1929 and eventually stabilizing at 132 in November 1936. However, given the semi-permanent structure of the MVSN there were few full-time serving officers, NCOs and Blackshirts; in 1930 there were only 1,089 active-duty officers out of a total of 7,227, while in 1939 across the whole of Italy there were 1,355 NCOs and 1,395 Blackshirts on active duty.

mobilized battalions of 115,000 all ranks. The Blackshirts provided the bulk of land forces in the Italo-Ethiopian War, with about 97,500 all ranks out of a grand total of 168,000 Italian soldiers sent to East Africa from Italy (who fought alongside locally raised colonial forces). Five Blackshirt divisions, each having three two-battalion *legioni*, were deployed in Eritrea, while the sixth division, deployed in Italian Somaliland, was mainly a volunteer unit formed within the framework of the Blackshirt organization, including those repatriated from abroad, World War I veterans, and students (it had four constituent *legioni*). The seventh division, deployed in Libya as a reserve, was the strongest with eight *legioni* and about 19,000 all ranks (see Table 1). All the divisions were disbanded shortly after the end of the war.

The end of the war against Ethiopia marked the start of a new phase for the Blackshirts. In November 1936 there were some 200 battalions, of which 102 were combat ones (78 with the army in Italy, 24 in the divisions in Libya and 30 *di copertura* – border defence – plus replacement and territorial ones). Italy's involvement in the Spanish Civil War saw the Blackshirts in battle again, but in a quite different fashion. No units were mobilized; instead, the Blackshirts served as a recruitment pool for the Corpo Truppe Volontarie (Volunteer Troops Corps), which included 29,000 of them. Organized in up to 36 independent *banderas* (battalions) grouped into short-lived divisions (later, mixed Spanish–Italian brigades), they were placed under army command after the setback at Guadalajara, which abruptly

A postcard from the 93[a] Legione 'Giglio Rosso' ('Red Lily') from Florence, reflecting the legacy of the Fascist *Squadre d'Azione*. The Blackshirts remained proud of their origins. This postcard shows a *Squadristi*-laden BL 18 lorry carrying them on a classic punitive raid against the enemies of Fascism. (Piero Crociani)

Table 1: Blackshirt units in the Italo-Ethiopian War, 1935–36	
1ª Divisione CCNN '23 Marzo'	Legioni 135ª (CXXXV, CXXXVIII), 192ª (CXCII, CXCV), 202ª (CCII, CCIV)
2ª Divisione CCNN '28 Ottobre'	Legioni 114ª (CXIV, CXV), 116ª (CXVI, CXXV), 180ª (CXXX, CXXXIV)
3ª Divisione CCNN '21 Aprile'	Legioni 230ª (CCXXX, CCXXXVI), 252ª (CCLII, CCLVI), 263ª (CCLXIII, CCLXIV)
4ª Divisione CCNN '3 Gennaio'	Legioni 101ª (CI, CII), 104ª (CIV, CXI), 215ª (CCXV, CCXX)
5ª Divisione CCNN '1 Febbraio'	Legioni 107ª (CVII, CLXXXVI), 128ª (CXXVIII, CXXIX), 142ª (CXLII, CCXLII)
6ª Divisione CCNN 'Tevere'	Legioni 219ª (CCXIX, CCCXIX), 220ª (CCI, CCXX), 221ª (CCXXI, CDXXI), 321ª (CCCXXI, DXXI)
7ª Divisione CCNN 'Cirene'	Legioni 198ª (CXCVIII, CCXL), 271ª (CCLXXI, CCLXXVI), 190ª (CXC, CCCXLI), 241ª (CCXLI, CCVII), 196ª (CXCVI, CCXLV), 219ª (CCXIX, CCXLIV), 267ª (CCLXVII, CCXLVIII), 352ª (CCCLII, CCCLXIII)
1º Gruppo Battaglioni (I–IV)	
6º Gruppo Battaglioni (III, LXXXI, LXXXII, CLXXI)	
Note: both the *legioni* and *battaglioni* had their original number increased by 100 (thus the 35ª Legione became the 135ª), with the exception of the two *gruppi battaglioni* (the first numbered its battalions in sequence, the second retained the original numbers)	

The war against Ethiopia between 1935 and 1936 was the first real test for the Blackshirts. This group ready to embark at Naples shows their age and status; many of them clearly are married and have children. The kneeling Blackshirt (possibly an NCO) wears two war merit promotion badges. (Laboratorio Storico-Iconografico della Facoltà di Scienze Politiche Università Roma Tre)

put an end to any illusion about a 'Fascist army'. Unsurprisingly, losses were proportionally higher than in Ethiopia, where 1,290 were killed in action (KIA); in Spain there were 1,461 KIA, 5,600 wounded in action (WIA) and about 280 missing in action (MIA). Despite the increase in the number of battalions, the army's opposition to strengthening the Blackshirt combat units, the latter's poor performances during the Spanish Civil War, and a general lack of interest on Mussolini's part eventually doomed any chance of their expansion.

In 1939 six battalions took part in the invasion of Albania. Four Blackshirt divisions, also consisting of army personnel, were mobilized in August for service in Libya, though in May 1940 one had to be disbanded to strengthen the other three (these divisions only had two *legioni* with three battalions each, see Table 2). In June 1940, when Italy entered World War II, there were only 72 Blackshirt combat battalions including 24 with the divisions in Libya and 44 with army divisions in Italy. Only 14 of the divisions actually had two battalions attached, while 16 only had one and 11 others had none. Only 28 battalions took part in the short-lived offensive across the Western Alps against France, attached to army divisions, without spectacular result. A major reorganization was started on 29 October 1940, just after the beginning of the ill-fated war against Greece; this envisaged a total of 39 *legioni* with 78 battalions (with 39 machine-gun companies and 39 replacement battalions) and a single two-battalion *legione* for the Aegean, plus six *legioni* and 18 battalions for the Blackshirt divisions in Libya. Up until Italy's surrender on 8 September 1943 up to 44 *legioni* (plus divisional ones) would be formed along with some 110 battalions (including independent ones, but with East Africa excluded). On paper it may have appeared to be an impressive force, but the reality was far from this.

1ª Divisione CCNN '23 Marzo'	219ª Legione (CXIX, CXIV, CXVIII), 233ª Legione (CXXIX, CXXXIII, CXLVIII)
2ª Divisione CCNN '28 Ottobre'	231ª Legione (CXXXI, CXXXII, CXXXV), 238ª Legione (CXXXVIII, CXL, CXLV)
3ª Divisione CCNN '21 Aprile' ¹	181ª Legione (LXXXI, LXXI, CII), 203ª (CIII, CX, CXLIII)
4ª Divisione CCNN '3 Gennaio'	270ª Legione (CLXX, CLXXII, CLXXIV), 250ª Legione (CL, CLIV, CLVI)

Notes:

¹ Disbanded May 1940, used to replenish the other three (LXXXI battalion replaced CLIV, which was disbanded).
The legion and battalion numbers were increased by 100, as per 1935–36.

World War II

The ill-fated war against Greece, which started on 28 October 1940, was the real test for Blackshirt units. Only three battalions were deployed in Albania when the Italians attacked (CIX with the Parma Division, CXLI with the Siena Division, and CLXVI with the Piemonte Division), but in the months that followed 20 legions were hurriedly mobilized and sent there to face the mounting threat of the Greek counteroffensive, often messing with the planned organization by switching the attachments of legions and battalions. The legions that fought against Greece were as follows: 15ª 'Leonessa' (XIV, XV battalions; with the Lupi di Toscana Division), 18ª (XIX, XXVII; Acqui), 24ª (XXIV, XXV; Cuneo), 26ª (VII, LIII; Legnano), 28ª (XI, XXVIII; Cagliari), 30ª (VI, XXX; Sforzesca), 36ª (XXXVI, LXXXIII; Modena), 45ª (XXXV, XLV; Brennero), 72ª (LXXII, CXI; Venezia), 80ª (XXVI, LXVII; Arezzo), 82ª (LXVIII, LXXXII; Ferrara), 105ª (CIV, CV; Cacciatori delle Alpi), 109ª (CIX, CXVI; Parma), 112ª (CXII, CXX; Forlì), 115ª (CXV, CXXI; Puglie), 136ª (CXXX, CXXXVI; Pinerolo), 141ª (CXLI, CLIII; Siena), 152ª (CLII, CLV; Bari), 164ª (CLXIII, CLXIV; Taro), and 166ª (CLXVI, CLXVII; Piemonte). An independent Raggruppamento Galbiati was also formed in December 1940 with three battalions (VIII, XVI, XXIX), while five other independent battalions fought in the area. Battlefield performances varied from poor to good, often with units being deployed at the front for a few weeks only.

A Blackshirt support company manning a 65/17 infantry gun in Ethiopia, 1936. Gun crews were formed using anti-aircraft militia (MACA) personnel. (Piero Crociani)

The Blackshirt LXXI Battaglione marching between Derna and Martuba on 12 October 1939. By June 1940 the four Blackshirt divisions deployed in Libya had been reduced to three. (Bruno Nunziati)

These were not as bad, however, as that of the Blackshirt divisions at Sidi Barrani in December 1940; here the '3 Gennaio' (disbanded on 10 December) was destroyed, while remnants of the '28 Ottobre' withdrew to Sollum and those of the '23 Marzo' to Bardia, where both were mauled and disbanded on 5 January 1941. Before the attack against Yugoslavia in April 1941 four other legions were moved to Albania: 23ᵃ (XX, XXIII; Casale), 49ᵃ (XL, XLIX; Marche), 92ᵃ (XCII, XCV; Firenze), and the 108ᵃ (CII, CVIII; Messina). Along with five of the *legioni* already in Albania these formed two combat groups: the Raggruppamento Diamanti (Legioni 28, 108, 115, 136, 152) and the Raggruppamento Biscaccianti (Legioni 80, 109; XCIII Battaglione). Eight *legioni* also took part in the war against Yugoslavia on the northern border: 5ᵃ (V, XXXIV; Ravenna), 17ᵃ (XVII, XVIII; Assietta), 73ᵃ (LXXIII, XLIV; Sassari), 75ᵃ (LXXV, LXXVI; Re), 88ᵃ (LXXXVIII, XCVI; Friuli), 89ᵃ (LXXXIX, XCVII; Bergamo), 98ᵃ (XCVIII, CXVII; Isonzo), 137ᵃ (CXXXIV, CXXXVII; Lombardia), along with 10 battalions.

A major reorganization took place in February–March 1941, before the conclusion of the Balkan campaign. Officially, seven battalions were disbanded (XIX, rebuilt, and XXVII of 18ᵃ Legione; CXLI, rebuilt, and CLIII of the 141ᵃ Legione; CXII of 112ᵃ Legione, CXXI of 115ᵃ Legione, CXXXVI of 136ᵃ Legione) along with 20 reserve ones, while ten Blackshirt battalions were rebuilt, having joined the divisions in Libya together with two of those from the battered

 VICE CAPO SQUADRA, 5ᵃ DIVISIONE CAMICIE NERE '18 FEBBRAIO', 1935

A Blackshirt *vice capo squadra* in Italian East Africa **(A)**, during the war against Ethiopia. He belongs to the 128ᵃ Legione 'Randaccio' from Vercelli, which unofficially adopted the edelweiss as its unit insignia **(4)**, part of the 5ᵃ Divisione Camicie Nere '18 Febbraio' **(3)**. Officers of the 5ᵃ Divisione had a special quote engraved on their daggers **(5)**, one of Mussolini's mottos: 'With heart and iron to the target'. The uniform is the Model 1935, with the characteristic cuffs, and the lapel badges **(2)** are the peacetime ones. The badge worn on the army topee **(1)** is a variation of the peacetime one first time adopted for the Blackshirts. This soldier is armed with a Carcano 91 rifle, whose 6.5mm ammunition was carried in the ammunition pouches attached to his belt **(8)**. The bayonet **(9)**, in its frog and scabbard, was carried suspended from the belt as well, along with the characteristic Blackshirt *pugnale* (dagger). His equipment also includes a much-needed canteen **(10)**, a haversack **(6)** with mess kit **(7)** and the new 1935 gas mask **(11)** carried in the new model gas mask bag **(12)**. The latter became a popular item that saw widespread use. It is interesting to note that the overall appearance and equipment of the Blackshirts in 1935 seems far superior to that of five years after this date, during World War II.

A group of Blackshirts just after the end of the short-lived Italo-French war; some are wearing French gendarme kepis, taken as war booty. The rank insignia and the territorial *legione* shield, as shown on the arm of the second Blackshirt from the right, are pre-war items. (Private collection)

legions. Also, in February the 93ª Legione (attached to the Livorno Division) was disbanded with its XCIII Battaglione becoming independent and the XCV used to replenish the 92ª Legione; the HQ was renamed and used to form the 195ª Legione along with two of the rebuilt battalions once they were in Libya (LXXI, LXXXI; in June 1942 these swapped with III and LXI), while two others were also used to replenish the battered legions (CII to the 108ª, CXLIII to the 90ª). In the months that followed the seven legions that fought in Greece were reduced to a single battalion (28ª with XXVIII, 36ª with XXXVI, 45ª with XXXV, 82ª with LXXXII, 105ª with CV, 109ª with CIX, 164ª with CLXIV), while two others were eventually disbanded (26ª with LIII, 36ª with XXXVI). Some legions were also detached from their divisions to be used in the Balkans for garrison and anti-partisan duties, such as the 2ª (I, II; Superga) and 86ª Legione (LXXXV,

The war against Greece in 1940–41 was a disaster for the Blackshirts; several battalions were lost. This photo shows a Blackshirt unit lined up after a battle; note their use of lightweight denim trousers and the mixture of black and grey-green shirts. (Archivio Centrale dello Stato, Rome)

Blackshirts marching along a muddy road somewhere in Albania during the war against Greece. The poor weather conditions led to improvised solutions such as the use of tents to shelter men and their equipment from rain. (Archivio Centrale dello Stato, Rome)

replaced by XCIV, LXXXVI; Cosseria) who were sent to Yugoslavia early in 1942. In contrast, the 55ª Legione (LX, LXXX; Granatieri di Sardegna) was sent back to Italy to form (on 1 August 1941), along with the 195ª Legione, the 30° Raggruppamento Camicie Nere; the former was replaced in its duties by the 95ª Legione (IX, CLXIII), itself later detached and sent back to Italy in late 1942.

By mid-September 1941 a total of 197 Blackshirt battalions of all types had been mobilized; 81 of them were either destroyed or disbanded (27 in Greece, 18 plus the six pre-war ones in Libya, and 30 in East Africa). Full mobilization had exhausted the established strength of 112,000, so older men and reservists were drafted into the combat battalions and four *Squadristi* battalions were also formed. The lack of manpower and dispersion of forces meant it was not

The single, short-lived Italian attack into Egypt in mid-September 1940 was halted at Sidi Barrani. This photo shows a group of Blackshirts charging forwards in the attack; the one to the right carries a Breda 30 automatic rifle. (Piero Crociani)

Blackshirts pulling a 20mm Breda Model 35 anti-aircraft gun section somewhere in Egypt. (Piero Crociani)

possible to make good the losses and attrition incurred, especially for the *legioni* attached to the divisions employed in garrison and anti-partisan duties. On 1 July 1942 there were 105 Blackshirt battalions on the rolls (27 in Italy, 35 in Yugoslavia plus eight in Montenegro, seven in Albania, nine in Greece, five in the Aegean, two in Libya and 11 on or en route to the Eastern Front); there were only 28 full-strength *legioni* plus ten single-battalion ones (making 71 battalions in the two-battalion *legioni* or the *gruppo battaglioni*, and 34 single ones). These were deployed as follows: on the Italian mainland and Sardinia, *legioni* 55ᵃ and 195ᵃ of the 30° Raggruppamento, 90ᵃ (XC, CXLIII; Cremona), 95ᵃ (detached), 152ᵃ (CLII, CLV; Bari), 176ᵃ (CLXXV, CLXXVI; Sabauda) and 177ᵃ (CLXXVII, CLXXVIII; Calabria); in Sicily or earmarked for the planned assault on Malta, *legioni* 17ᵃ, 88ᵃ, 171ᵃ (CLXVIII, CLXXI; Aosta) and 173ᵃ (CLXIX, CLXXIII; Napoli); in Yugoslavia, *legioni* 2ᵃ, 23ᵃ, 49ᵃ, 73ᵃ, 75ᵃ, 89ᵃ, 98ᵃ, 105ᵃ, 108ᵃ and 137ᵃ, plus 72ᵃ, 82ᵃ, 86ᵃ and 164ᵃ in Montenegro; in Albania 18ᵃ, 80ᵃ, 92ᵃ, 109ᵃ and 115ᵃ; in Greece, *legioni* 28ᵃ,

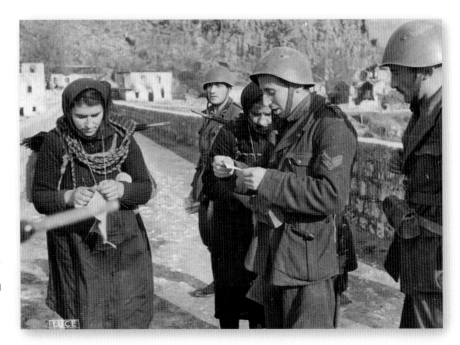

A Blackshirt roadblock somewhere in Montenegro, 1942. Following the conclusion of the Balkan campaign, many Blackshirt units were employed in garrison and anti-partisan duties in the area. (Archivio Centrale dello Stato, Rome)

Blackshirts patrolling in a town in Yugoslavia, probably in 1943. Note the 9mm Beretta 38 machine pistols. (Private collection)

45ª, 112ª, 136ª and 166ª; in the Aegean, *legioni* 24ª, 141ª and 201ª (CCI, CCCI; Regina), plus the four legions already on the Eastern Front or earmarked for it. By January 1943 the situation had changed little; there were now 110 battalions (22 in Italy and 10 in Corsica, 33 in Yugoslavia and eight in Montenegro, six in Albania, 14 in Greece, four in the Aegean, two in Libya, and 11 on the Eastern Front) mostly grouped in larger units following the general reorganization undertaken by the legions in the Balkans on the model of the 'M' units. In Greece three *gruppi battaglioni* were formed with two Blackshirt battalions and a heavy weapons one ('L'Aquila' with CXX, CXXX from 112ª and 136ª Legioni plus CCXXX; 'Etna' with CLXVI, CLXVII from 166ª Legione and CCLXVI; 'Po' with XX, XXIII from 23ª Legione and CCXXIII), while in Yugoslavia a Raggruppamento 21 Aprile was formed with the 2ª Legione plus IV and CCXV Squadristi Blackshirt Battaglione 'Nizza', formed on 1 June 1942 from XV Battaglione and named after Garibaldi's birthplace.

The Gruppo Battaglioni 'M' 'Tagliamento' departing for the Eastern Front, summer 1941. (Archivio Centrale dello Stato, Rome)

Luogotenente Generale Enrico Francisci, commander until November 1942 of the Raggruppamento 23 Marzo; he was to die in July 1943 during the fight for Sicily. On his chest are two war merit promotions and the eagle denoting staff officer status. (Archivio Centrale dello Stato, Rome)

The 'M' battalions

While the bulk of the Blackshirt units supported the army in garrison and anti-partisans duties, a selective reorganization took place with the creation of the 'M' (for Mussolini) battalions, which produced an 'elite' from the existing units. In early 1941 there had been talk of creating a new Blackshirt division along the lines of the Waffen-SS, but nothing came of it. The first 'M' battalions were officially created on 1 October 1941 from those battalions that distinguished themselves during the war against Greece and were quoted in the armed forces' bulletin, namely those of the Raggruppamento Galbiati that fought at Maritzai in February–March 1941 (VIII, XVI, XXIX), and those of 15ª Legione 'Leonessa' (XIV, XV) who distinguished themselves in February 1941. The title of 'M' battalions was also conferred in the field to the battalions of the 63ª Legione sent to the Eastern Front in June 1941 (LXIII, LXXIX; attached: LXIII, army heavy weapons). By spring 1942 other battalions were to follow; in Italy four 'M' battalions formed the Gruppo Battaglioni CCNN da Sbarco (XLII, XLIII, L, LX; envisaged by the October 1940 reorganization) for the planned assault on Malta, which actually only landed (unopposed) in Corsica in November 1942 along with three *legioni* (55ª, 88ª and 90ª) – two battalions (XLII, L) of which were sent to southern France early in 1943. The majority of the 'M' battalions – 11 out of the 22 formed – were sent to the Eastern Front

A flame-thrower team from the 1ª Divisione Corazzata 'M' training near Rome, spring 1943. These Blackshirts, dressed in lightweight denim uniform, are practising with a German Model 41 Flammenwerfer. (Archivio Centrale dello Stato, Rome)

and fully reorganized; in spring 1942 three *legioni* were used to form new *gruppi battaglioni* which were then used to create two battle groups deployed with the Italian army sent to the Soviet Union in late summer. The Raggruppamento CCNN 3 Gennaio was made up of the Gruppo battaglioni CCNN M 'Tagliamento' (formed from the 63ª Legione) and the 'Montebello' (VI, XXX, XII heavy weapons) from the 30ª Legione; while the Raggruppamento CCNN '23 Marzo' was made up of the *gruppo battaglioni* CCNN M 'Leonessa' (XIV, XV, XXXVIII heavy weapons), formerly the 15ª Legione, and the 'Valle Scrivia' (V, XXXIV, XLI heavy weapons), formerly the

Germany supplied a dozen each of the Panzer IV Ausf. G and Panzer III Ausf. N tanks to the 1ª Divisione Corazzata 'M', whose insignia can be seen on the turret of this Panzer IV Ausf. G. (Archivio Centrale dello Stato, Rome)

5ª Legione. Six other 'M' battalions fought against the partisans in Yugoslavia (VIII, XVI, XXIX, LXXI and LXXXI formerly of the 195ª Legione, LXXXV plus the Confinario border battalion) while X, deployed in Sicily, was sent to Tunisia in December 1942 and destroyed there in May 1943.

As the Blackshirts' combat elite, the 'M' battalions would suffer the most from the setbacks on the Eastern Front in winter 1942–43. Having suffered heavy losses, the remnants of the *gruppi battaglioni* were brought back to Italy and used to create the 1ª Divisione Corazzata Camicie Nere 'M'. This 5,700-strong unit began training in May, but was only formed as Mussolini's bodyguard on 25 June 1943 following the delivery of 24 tanks, 12 self-propelled guns, 24 88mm anti-aircraft guns and 24 flame-throwers from Germany (see Table 3). The fact that it did not react to Mussolini's downfall on 25 July 1943 came to symbolize the failure of the Blackshirts as a military expression of Fascism.

Table 3: 1ª Divisione Corazzata Camicie Nere 'M' (1st Blackshirt Armoured Division)	
Gruppo Carri 'Leonessa' (tank battalion)	
Gruppo battaglioni CCNN 'M' 'Tagliamento'	(XLI, LXIII, LXXIX)
Gruppo battaglioni CCNN 'M' 'Montebello'	(VI, XII, XXX)
Reggimento Artiglieria 'Valle Scrivia' (artillery regiment)	(I, II)
Combat engineer battalion, sappers and communications, supplies and medical services	

Blackshirt unit organization

Given their semi-permanent structure, which brought units into existence only after their mobilization, the Blackshirts' unit capabilities were limited in many ways. They were basically light infantry battalions grouped into regiments (*legioni*) and were only rarely put together into larger brigade- or division-sized units. In the case of the latter, army personnel would also be needed to provide specialist units like artillery, communications, engineers, services and headquarters. The Blackshirt territorial *legioni* often lacked proper barracks, and those available could only accommodate individual weapons and a limited amount of ammunition. Uniforms, weapons, ammunition and equipment were

The Divisione '23 Marzo' in tent camp in Ethiopia, 1936. This was the first time that Italian armed units would have been supplied by air. (Piero Crociani)

provided on mobilization. The first *legioni* to be mobilized in 1923 were in fact battalion-strength units each made up of three to six 354-men *coorti*, themselves made up of three *centurie*. Thus a single *legione* could be 1,000 to 2,100 strong, though actual strength rarely exceeded the lower figure.

The war against Ethiopia in 1935–36 marked the high point of the Blackshirts' field organization. Following the creation of the Blackshirt battalions the *legione* was now the equivalent of a regiment with two battalions, each some 890 strong. The Blackshirt divisions sent to Ethiopia were made up of three *legioni* each, one of which also had a machine-gun company, a field gun battery and, sometimes, even a flame-thrower section. They also included a Blackshirt machine-gun battalion, an army artillery battalion, two Blackshirt replacements battalions, a mixed Army–Blackshirt special engineer company (including communications and sappers), and divisional services. The total strength was 366 officers, 369 NCOs and 9,962 other ranks (including Blackshirt and army personnel, mainly in divisional HQ and services). Weapons included some 9,500 rifles, 180 automatic rifles, 98 machine guns, and 24 65mm field guns; vehicles were a sore point, with each division having only eight cars, 94 lorries, and 1,700 pack animals. With its four *legioni* the 6ª Division 'Tevere' (Tiber) had 456 officers and 14,111 other ranks, while the two *gruppo battaglioni* (each with four battalions) were 3,541 strong. Such an organization was not to be matched again; the Blackshirt divisions formed in 1939–40 only had two legions, each with three battalions plus one mortar company and one gun battery, one Blackshirt machine-gun battalion, one anti-tank company, a three-battalion (*gruppi*) field artillery regiment, a mixed engineers battalion, and divisional services. Less than 10,000 strong, the actual number of Blackshirts therein was limited since every *legione* was only 2,271 strong (94 officers, 84 NCOs, 2,093 Blackshirts), with 734 in each battalion (29 officers, 27 NCOs and 678 Blackshirts) plus 148 all ranks in the machine-gun company. Armament included 81 automatic rifles (27 in each battalion), 36 machine guns (12 in each MG company), and 27 45mm mortars (nine in each battalion). Army personnel predominated in the gun-armed units (gun batteries, anti-tank companies, field artillery regiments), and provided the engineer battalion and divisional services.

Table 4: The Blackshirt *legione* and its *battaglioni*, 1940

	Officers	NCOs	Other ranks	Assault rifles	Machine guns	45mm mortars
Legione HQ	11	9	84			
Blackshirt battalion (total)	18	29	474	24		9
HQ	6	8	96			
1–3 companies	12	21	378	24		9
1–2 Blackshirt battalions	36	58	1006	48		18
MG company	5	9	207		12	
Totals	**52**	**76**	**1,306**	**48**	**12**	**18**

The *legioni* attached to army divisions were stronger, though actual established strengths often diverged from their paper ones. Each *legione* had two Blackshirt battalions (each with three companies) and a machine-gun company. It was 1,434 strong with 52 officers, 76 NCOs and 1,306 Blackshirts with 48 automatic rifles, 12 machine guns, and 18 45mm mortars. A single Blackshirt battalion was 521 strong with 18 officers, 29 NCOs, and 474 Blackshirts armed with 24 automatic rifles and nine 45mm mortars (see Table 4). Also, every legion was to include a replacement battalion (*complementi*) with two companies having 11 officers (four in each company), 17 NCOs (seven) and 264 Blackshirts (107), armed with 24 automatic rifles (12 in each company), and two machine guns. However, these would practically disappear at the conclusion of the Balkan campaigns in spring 1941. As events on the battlefield made clear, neither the divisional organization nor the attachment of *legioni* to the army divisions were suitable solutions. Lacking both specialized personnel and barracks, the Blackshirt divisions could only be formed with the army's contribution, which greatly hampered their combat effectiveness in the field. Likewise, attached *legioni* proved wholly inadequate; weaker than their army counterparts, they could not be used like other army infantry regiments and were eventually employed as pseudo-reconnaissance units or to make good for the lack of other units. The creation of ad hoc combat groups like the Raggruppamento used in the war against Greece to regroup Blackshirt battalions and *legioni* proved to be an ideal solution, one brought to fruition in the creation of the *gruppo battaglioni* to replace the *legione*. The first to be formed – the 63[a] Legione in June 1941, later to become the *gruppo battaglioni* Camicie Nere 'M' 'Tagliamento' – was in fact an impromptu solution, since it had, along with its two Blackshirt battalions, an army heavy weapons battalion (*armi d'accompagnamento*).

Only in spring–summer 1942, following the creation of the 'M' Gruppo battaglioni 'Montebello', 'Leonessa', and 'Valle Scrivia' with their own heavy-weapons battalions formed from existing Blackshirts ones, did the new organization take shape. Later the same year three other *gruppo battaglioni* were formed, in Greece ('L'Aquila', 'Etna', and 'Po'). If the *gruppo battaglioni* was a development of the former *legione* organization, the Raggruppamento Camicie Nere formed with twin *gruppo battaglioni* in Russia were to be the largest Blackshirt units deployed on the battlefield since 1940. These brigade-sized units ranked as the elite of the Blackshirts, being allotted both motor vehicles and adequate weaponry, including anti-tank guns. A *gruppo battaglioni* was on paper 1,593 strong (69 officers, 93 NCOs, 1,297 Blackshirts, and 134 drivers), had 36 motorcycles, four cars and 124 light lorries, and was armed with 48 automatic rifles, 24 machine

	Officers	NCOs	Other ranks	Drivers	Motorcycles	Cars	Lorries	Assault rifles	Machine guns	45mm mortars	81mm mortars	47/32 AT guns
HQ	10	8	77	11	7	1	8					
'M' Blackshirt battalion	22	33	489	43	10	1	41	24	12	9		
1–2 Blackshirt battalions	44	66	978	86	20	2	82	48	24	18		
Heavy weapons battalion	15	19	242	37	9	1	34				6	8
Totals	**69**	**93**	**1,297**	**134**	**36**	**4**	**124**	**48**	**24**	**18**	**6**	**8**

guns, 18 45mm mortars, six 81mm mortars, and eight 47mm (47/32) anti-tank guns, the last two in the heavy weapons battalion's mortar and gun companies. These 'M' Blackshirt battalions, made up of three Blackshirt companies and a machine-gun company, were stronger and better equipped than the others, with 587 men (22 officers, 33 NCOs, 489 Blackshirts, and 43 drivers), 41 lorries, 24 automatic rifles, nine 45mm mortars, and 12 machine guns (see Table 5).

In contrast, the personnel shortage brought revisions to the established strength of the average Blackshirt *legioni* and battalions. The overall strength of a *legione* (the organization of which remained unchanged) would fall to 1,356 with 51 officers, 75 NCOs, and 1,230 Blackshirts, though the weapons allowance did not change (48 automatic rifles, 12 machine guns, and 18 45mm mortars) and a degree of motorization was introduced with two motorcycles, one car, and five light lorries added to the more customary 206 mules. A more common Blackshirt battalion was now 494 strong with 18 officers, 29 NCOs, and 447 Blackshirts, still armed with 24 automatic rifles and nine 45mm mortars (see Table 6). The organization of the amphibious 'M' battalions (*da sbarco* – seaborne landing) was unique; each of the four existing ones, with

Religion had a formal role to play in the Blackshirt units, just as it did in the Fascist regime. Here a field mass is being held, with a trumpeter included. (Piero Crociani)

Table 6: Wartime strength of Blackshirt *legione* and *battaglione*, 1941–43

	Officers	NCOs	Other ranks	Pack animals	Motor cycles	Cars	Lorries	Assault rifles	Machine guns	45mm mortars
Legione HQ	10	8	84	13	2	1	1			
Blackshirt battalion	18	29	474	76			2	24		9
1–2 Blackshirt battalions	36	58	948	152			4	48		18
MG company	5	9	198	41					12	
Totals	**51**	**75**	**1,230**	**206**	**2**	**1**	**5**	**48**	**12**	**18**

Table 7: Blackshirt 'M' Gruppo battaglioni da sbarco, March 1942

	Officers	NCOs	Other ranks	Assault rifles	Machine guns	45mm mortars	47/32 guns	Motorcycles
HQ	13	4	80					
1–4 battalions	96	204	2504	108	36	36		
47/32 gun company	6	9	133				8	
Service company	7	14	261		6			
Totals	**122**	**231**	**2,978**	**108**	**42**	**36**	**8**	**3**

three companies, was 701 strong (24 officers, 51 NCOs, and 626 Blackshirts) and had 27 automatic rifles, nine machine guns, and nine 45mm mortars. As per the March 1942 establishment, the Gruppo Battaglioni Camicie Nere 'M' da sbarco, which also included one anti-tank and one service company, was to be 3,331 strong and armed with a grand total of 108 automatic rifles, 42 machine guns, 36 45mm mortars, and eight 47/32 anti-tank guns (see Table 7).

The moment every soldier in the field awaits: the post from home. (Private collection)

WEAPONS

When tested on the field of battle, Blackshirt units performed with mixed results. Their overall performance during the 1935–36 war was good, much less so during the Spanish Civil War and in the early stages of World War II, when only some *legioni* and battalions proved themselves competent in battle. Later on, Blackshirt units gave good accounts of themselves on the Eastern Front, and in the Balkans where, in a sense, they felt at home fighting against Tito's partisans. The main shortcomings among the Blackshirt units were their lack of service elements and their armament, which they shared with the army.

One of the most common weapons used by the Blackshirts was the 9mm Beretta 34 automatic pistol, for officers and those soldiers armed with automatic guns; it was small and reliable, but not very effective. Rifles, all of them Mannlicher Carcano 6.5mm, ranged from the long-barrelled rifle model 91 with bayonet to the smaller model 91, either with or without the folding bayonet. Their small calibre and lack of power made them largely inferior to those of most of their enemies, at least after the war against Ethiopia. The Breda model 30 automatic rifle was innovative for its time, roughly comparable to the American Browning Automatic Rifle, though not quite as effective; it used the same 6.5mm round as the rifles but this time inserted in a fixed cartridge clip of 20 rounds, which greatly hampered its effectiveness in spite of the rate of fire, which was 400–500 rounds per minute. Machine guns varied from the water-cooled 6.5mm Fiat-Revelli model 14, largely used in 1935–36, to the modern 8mm Breda model 37 (which could fire 450 rounds per minute, though this was hampered by the use of 20-round ammunition clips) and the inferior 6.5mm Fiat-Revelli model 35.

From 1942 onwards, a few of the 'M' battalions (the amphibious ones and those sent to the Eastern Front) were also armed with the highly reliable and effective 9mm Beretta machine pistol; this was only issued to officers and NCOs. Hand grenades (OTO model 35, SRCM model 35, and Breda model 35) were light, weighing 200–300g, but were not very effective. The 45mm Brixia model 35 mortar was a much better weapon, actually more effective than the heavier 81mm mortar model 35. Field guns used included the 65mm infantry gun 65/17, a solid weapon but dating back to World War I, and the 47mm anti-tank gun 47/32 model 37, which, in 1941–42, was obsolete.

B **1ª DIVISIONE CAMICIE NERE '23 MARZO', LIBYA, SPRING 1940**
The four Blackshirt divisions deployed in Libya at the end of 1939 (reduced to three in May 1940) were a kind of hangover from the Blackshirt divisions formed in 1935 for the war against Ethiopia. Until the summer of 1940 the continental grey-green uniforms (and often shirts too, replacing the unsuitable black ones) were still quite common, especially because they were more comfortable in winter in certain areas of Libya. The tropical uniform had the same shape as the model 1940 continental wartime uniform, but it was made of lightweight, khaki-greenish cotton. The *sahariana* tropical uniform was widely appreciated, though still mostly used by officers only; it was available both in the pre-1940 and 1940 models (there were minor differences between them). Here, the *sotto capo manipolo* (second lieutenant) is wearing the *sahariana*; together with a *primo capo squadra* (lance sergeant), he is watching a group of Blackshirts improvising their supper having returned from their duties. The Blackshirts, like their Italian Army counterparts, had no separate arrangements for the rank and file mess; this was only available to officers and NCOs. The topee was the most common form of headgear in Libya in 1940 (steel helmets were rarely used), though the Blackshirts preferred to wear their fez when off duty.

RECRUITMENT AND ENLISTMENT

Only a relatively small number of Blackshirts joined combat units, which were also formed on a volunteer basis (however, only those aged between 26 and 36 could enlist, for a period of ten years, and were eventually drafted if the army made them available – the *Alpini* mountain infantry were excluded from this). In practice, the Blackshirts would only rarely find themselves on active duty, as the lack of barracks restricted their service to periods spent in the field. This was the case for the three *legioni* mobilized in 1923; they were simple enough to raise, given the availability of a large number of World War I veterans and young men. Similarly, in 1935–36 the strength of the Blackshirt combat units expanded from 20,000 to 115,000 for the war against Ethiopia, thanks to the large number of available volunteers originally not part of the battalions. However, the main shortcoming of combat Blackshirts was the age of those recruited; the army drafted men aged 21–24, while most Blackshirts were 26–45. An examination of a sample of 40,000 Blackshirts sent to eastern Africa shows a quarter were aged 31–36 and half 26–30. In general, NCOs were older (50 per cent were aged over 35, and 22 per cent over 40), while Blackshirt officers were younger than most of their soldiers and NCOs and than their army counterparts as well. The rapid disbandment of the Blackshirt divisions shortly after the end of the war marked the beginning of a new phase, coinciding with the beginning of Italian involvement in the Spanish Civil War, which in turn put further strain on the Blackshirts. The influx of new volunteers created a divide between the combat battalions, made up of volunteers aged 26–36, and the territorial battalions, made up of older men aged up to 55. In July 1939 the army, which was reluctant to allow an excessive growth in the numbers of Blackshirts, set a ceiling of 142,000 volunteers to be made available for the *legioni*. However, in June 1940 the total established strength of the Blackshirt battalions was only 112,000, and the actual strength of mobilized units was less than 42,000. Not included in these figures are the 30 Blackshirt battalions deployed in Italian East Africa, whose strength rose to 26,000 thanks to locally recruited volunteers (four, later reduced to two, battalions would be raised in Libya in the same way).

One of the most vital supplies in the desert – water. Here the Blackshirts are filling up any kind of container they can, including a demijohn intended for wine. (Archivio Centrale dello Stato, Rome)

Full mobilization would follow immediately after the ill-fated attack against Greece, which, two weeks after its start, saw the Greeks counterattacking and the Italians racing to build up their forces in Albania. Hurriedly raised and sent to the front, the *legioni* suffered considerably. Heavier losses were inflicted on the three Blackshirt units deployed in Egypt, which were shattered by the British offensive of December 1940. In September 1941 a summary report estimated that total Blackshirt losses amounted to 81 battalions (including the 30 in Italian East Africa); some 40 per cent of the total strength of 112,000 had been lost as well, plus over ten per cent due to wounds, injuries, illness, or age-related withdrawal. Since the Blackshirt recruitment pool of those aged 26–36 was practically exhausted, the chief of staff of the MVSN, Galbiati, appealed to the

Blackshirt units often lacked service elements, like the field kitchen shown here; such elements were provided by the division, *legioni*, or battalion that the units were attached to. (Private collection)

chief of the Italian general staff, Generale Cavallero, for a major reorganization of the combat units. However, only stopgap measures were implemented. One was the transfer of 4,000 former Blackshirts aged over 40 from the army, which received younger recruits in return; another was the reorganization of five battalions (all deployed in Yugoslavia: VII, LXVIII, LXXXIII, CXII and the rebuilt CLXX) with reservists, which were renamed *Squadristi Battaglioni* because they were now largely made up of veterans of the 'Fascist revolution'. Much more effective was the decision to allow the transfer of 4,000 19-year-old *giovani Fascisti* (members of the Fascist youth organization) into the Blackshirt ranks; they first served in the MACA, before being drafted by the army in April 1942 and, after three months' training, used to replenish the ranks of the new 'M' battalions sent to the Eastern Front in the months that followed.

A Blackshirt unit attacking a Russian position in the Dniepr basin, summer 1942. Italian tactics envisaged the infantry dashing forward under cover of Breda 30 automatic rifle fire, before throwing their hand grenades in the final yards of their attack. (Archivio Centrale dello Stato, Rome)

The Blackshirt's basic weapons included the model 91 rifle and the barely effective OTO (Odero Terni Orlando) hand grenade. (Archivio Centrale dello Stato, Rome)

None of these measures could prevent the impending crisis that was already evident by July 1942; some 6,470 Blackshirts were missing from the established strength of 63,800 for the 99 existing battalions (plus the six *Squadristi*) and forecasted losses for the year to follow would also require another 12,000 replacements to replenish units on the Eastern Front (6,000), and in the Balkans (3,000), Greece (1,200), Albania (1,200), and Italy (600). The army's response to the Blackshirts' request was to suggest the disbandment of some battalions, before it agreed to transfer another 4,000 *giovani Fascisti* and, eventually, in November 1942, to allow army personnel that in peacetime had been members of the MVSN to transfer to the Blackshirts. The creation on 20 November 1942 of Blackshirt replacement battalions proved optimistic, since, due to the large number of restrictions imposed (those serving in combat units and specialists were excluded), few men would eventually be transferred. The same was to happen in early 1943 when, out of the 10,000 *giovani Fascisti* promised by the army, only 3,000 were actually transferred to the Blackshirts from the class of 1923. When the class of 1924 was called to duty in May and July 1943, the army put aside all interest in supplying personnel to the Blackshirts.

C

RAGGRUPPAMENTO GALBIATI, GREECE/ALBANIA, WINTER 1940–41
The ill-fated Italian attack against Greece in October 1940 represented a crucial test for the Blackshirts, one that was even more challenging than the first phase of the North African campaign. Like their army counterparts, the Blackshirt legions and battalions were hurriedly thrown into battle, lacking training, proper clothing and equipment, and often supplies as well. However, the first attempts at consolidating the Blackshirt units into larger *raggruppamenti* (groupings) took place here, foreshadowing their future deployment on the Eastern Front. The first to be formed, in December 1940, was the Raggruppamento Galbiati, named (like the others) after its commander, which included the VIII, XVI and XXIX battalions. Between March and April 1941 two other *raggruppamenti* were formed to take part in the attack on Yugoslavia; the Raggruppamento Biscaccianti (with the 80ª and 109ª Legione and the XCIII battalion) and the Raggruppamento Diamanti, which included the 28ª, 108ª, 115ª, 136ª, and 152ª Legione. Raggruppamento Galbiati would distinguish itself in the battle of Maritzai in February–March 1941 and, on 1 October 1941, its battalions, along with those of the 15ª Legione 'Leonessa', became the first to be transformed into 'M' ones. During the war against Greece the lack of suitable winter clothing greatly affected the Italians. This illustration shows a mixture of Blackshirt officers and other ranks advancing forwards, including a Breda 37 HMG team to the right; all the troops are wearing the inadequate model 1934 greatcoat. The officer in the centre is holding a model 35 OTO hand grenade, which was effective only within a ten-yard radius.

The innovative 6.5mm Breda 30 automatic rifle was widely used by the Blackshirts, but it was not a very effective weapon. (Archivio Centrale dello Stato, Rome)

In contrast to the rank and file, filling the cadres was not as problematic. Until 1936 there was only one single NCO rank (*capo squadra*), as so few were needed. The NCO recruitment pool was only partly filled by army veterans; instead a large number of them came from the Blackshirts' ranks. Thus, in 1940, 2,590 NCOs out of the 4,250 who served in the 1935–36 war against Ethiopia were Blackshirts; 1,606 of them were World War I veterans. An NCO school was set up at Mirandola, later moved to Livorno (Leghorn) and then to Rome; however, promotion to *vice capo squadra* (the lowest NCO rank) was simply granted by passing a test, with a select few being promoted further. After five years of active service duty NCOs could be commissioned as officers, though, following the Italian practice, a secondary school diploma was required for this. Few were required, however, since the Blackshirts had plenty of officers.

In the early years high-ranking officers in the Blackshirts mainly came from ex-army personnel (particularly colonels and generals), while most of the *centurioni* and *capi manipolo* were former *Squadristi* and also ex-army officers (in 1923, only 44 *centurioni* out of 227 were not ex-army). Later on, the bulk of the Blackshirt junior officers was provided by army reserve lieutenants (those holding secondary-school diplomas could be drafted into the Italian armed forces as substantive junior officers in peacetime) who joined the MVSN. The large number of units and men employed in the war against Ethiopia and in the Spanish Civil War led to extensive combat promotions (for leadership skills or bravery), which ensured the Blackshirts had an adequate number of experienced senior officers and *centurioni* who

The watercooled 6.5mm Fiat-Revelli Model 14 was widely used during the war against Ethiopia and thereafter. The ritual of blessing the weapons was a popular one in the Italian armed forces. (Laboratorio Storico-Iconografico della Facoltà di Scienze Politiche Università Roma Tre)

were well suited to command. In 1940 the new regulations, reflecting the actual situation, stated that only ex-armed forces officers could be Blackshirt officers assuming that they were members of the Fascist party and were not older than 35 for the junior officers, 40 for *centurioni*, or 45 for high-ranking officers.

Nevertheless, in 1942 the Blackshirt battalions fell short of junior officers, for three simple reasons: a good deal of them (some 15,000 reserve officers) had been recalled to duty by the armed forces, the army would no longer discharge its substantive officers as they were now needed by combat units, and both losses and promotions were taking their toll. Eventually the army consented to transfer 500 of its junior, former Blackshirt, officers, though only 74 of them actually applied to do so. In December 1942 the Blackshirts sought permission to create an officers' academy for 400 university students who had already completed the MVSN's equivalent of an officer training course. However, in January 1943 the request was denied, and eventually a three-month officer training course was created for those rank and file Blackshirts and NCOs serving in the battalions who had shown themselves to possess the necessary qualities (and also possessed a secondary-school diploma). The army's opposition delayed the start of this course to 1 April 1943; 183 decorated NCOs took part; by mid-July (shortly before Mussolini's downfall) 179 had completed it, and were subsequently commissioned and sent to the battalions.

The 6.5mm Fiat-Revelli Model 35 machine gun is shown here being carried on a lorry in the Western Desert, 1940. (Archivio Centrale dello Stato, Rome)

Mules were widely used by Blackshirt units, which often lacked adequate vehicle support. They would prove to be a highly effective means of transportation in difficult terrain. Note the grey-green shirt and sweater and the infantry badge (probably 'borrowed' from an army unit) on the helmet of this Blackshirt. (Archivio Centrale dello Stato, Rome)

TRAINING

Inadequate training dogged the Italian armed forces throughout the period under discussion, and the Blackshirts were no exception to this – particularly given their semi-permanent nature, and the lack of barracks and training facilities. Until the mid-1930s Italian infantry training was largely influenced by the experiences of World War I, with defence predominating, following the example of the French army. From the mid-1930s, however, Italian doctrine was largely influenced by the notion of a war of short duration, which stressed and emphasized attack.

Blackshirt training was almost identical to that of the Italian standard infantry, which was similarly hampered by a lack of resources – despite the claims of the Fascist regime's bombastic propaganda. A good deal of the training comprised basic drill and long marches, with few live-firing exercises characterized by the limited amount of rounds available (particularly for the automatic and heavy weapons). Summer field exercises involving several units would be held, though with little reference to inter-arms and inter-service cooperation. Apart from the relatively short periods of mobilization and war, most Blackshirt activity was restricted to attending official ceremonies, which meant the emphasis was put on formal drill. The lack of barracks and shortage of weapons (at the end of 1939 there only were about 152,000 rifles, 2,400 automatic rifles and four machine guns for the 300,000 men of the MVSN) made it practically impossible to train the Blackshirt battalions. However, most of the Blackshirts had gained experience during their compulsory military service, or had fought in combat, which made up for the most pressing of the deficiencies.

The dearth of training came to the fore as early as 1932, when some of the Blackshirt battalions took part in army manoeuvres. The creation of the Blackshirt divisions, which included army personnel, made more comprehensive training vital. This task was undertaken by the army, which decided to start again from scratch with an intensive programme divided into three different phases: firstly, individual training, which included the usual drill plus basic firearms training, followed by platoon and squad drill, and theory lectures; secondly, firing exercises, field reconnaissance, and technical training for artillery observers, radio and telephone operators, etc.; thirdly,

D

SENIORE, 'M' BATTALION, 1942

Officially created on 1 October 1941, the 'M' (for Mussolini) Battalions were a true elite among the Blackshirts; only 22 were created. This *seniore* (major) **(A)** is wearing the characteristic wartime lapel badges (shorter than the peacetime ones) for the 'M' Battalions with the red 'M' (taken from Mussolini's signature) intersected by the *fascio* **(3)**. The black sidecap, with the insignia for Blackshirt officers **(1)**, was only used for a short time in 1941 an 1942. This officer is a *Squadrista* – a member of the Blackshirts before Mussolini's rise to power in October 1922 – as shown by the civilian badge worn on the chest **(2)** and the red stripes on his cuffs (other Blackshirts wore a red *fascio* on their lapels, **(4)**). Other items shown include an engraved dagger **(5)**, the Arditi sleeve badge **(6)**, a map case **(7)**, a Beretta 34 pistol **(8)**, and holster **(9)**. This officer has won several decorations during his period of service **(10)**: from top right to bottom left, we see the ribbons of a silver medal, a military war cross, the order of saints Maurizio and Lazzaro, the order of Italy's crown (*ordine della corona d'Italia*), a World War I service medal showing two years' service, an Italian East Africa 1935–36 war medal, a Spanish Civil War service medal, a cross for long service in the Blackshirt battalions (enhanced), and a two-year World War II service medal. The other insignia shown **(11)** include, top to bottom, the chest badges worn by members of the battaglioni Camicie Nere da sbarco, that of the 82ª Legione Camicie Nere 'Benito Mussolini', of the 92ª and 93ª Legioni, of the 113ª Legione 'dell'Urbe', and of the Raggruppamento Camicie Nere Galbiati, which fought during the war against Greece.

1

2

3

11

4

5

6

A

7

8

9

10

Although not a particularly useful form of training, the German-inspired goose-step parade march was often executed. These 'M' Blackshirts are on parade in 1942. (Count Ernesto G. Vitetti)

company- and battalion-level training in simulated battle conditions including live-firing, plus lectures on war in a tropical environment, the enemy, and fieldcraft. Officers also had an extra hour of daily lectures given by their battalion commander. Field marches, which coordinated battalions into *legioni* and *legioni* into divisions, was the final phase prior to the regrouping of the Blackshirt divisions in the area around Naples, from whence they would embark to an overseas destination.

Such training, which continued while in the field, proved more than adequate against the Ethiopians, who lacked training, weapons, artillery, tanks, and aeroplanes. The main challenges were provided by logistical issues and the terrain, which were overcome thanks to hard work; the Blackshirts' shovels and picks would provide Ethiopia with a road network that is still in use over 70 years later. The experience of the Spanish Civil War would be quite different, however; the Blackshirts were hurriedly sent to Spain without pre-organization (units were formed on the spot) and following only rapid basic training. Their

Newly formed 'M' Blackshirt battalions were the first ones to be fully trained at two camps built on purpose in Rome during autumn 1941; one at Centocelle and one at Trastevere, in the Porta Portese area now known for the flea market. (Archivio Centrale dello Stato, Rome)

A Blackshirt explains how to use a rangefinder to the MVSN chief of staff, Galbiati; the former wears denim fatigue dress, and the officers are wearing black caps. (Count Ernesto G. Vitetti)

experience helped the Blackshirts obtain success at first on the field, as at Malaga, but there was soon a rude awakening at the battle of Guadalajara. The Blackshirt units shrank in numbers, while in Italy ten short training courses were held, attended by 572 officers who were subsequently sent to Spain to help make good the situation. This was one of the first duties of the newly formed training detachment of the MVSN's general staff (Ufficio Addestramento del Comando Generale della MVSN), which in the meantime also started a series of training courses for Blackshirt officers. Held at the army schools at Civitavecchia near Rome, these included two training courses for battalion commanders, and two for machine-gunners and for officers training personnel to fire the 45mm mortar. It is worth noting that in this period the Blackshirt battalions rarely took part in army field exercises and manoeuvres – four battalions each year between 1936 and 1938, and only six in 1939 took part in the field exercises of the newly formed Armata del Po (army mechanized reserve). The *legioni* were a little more active; in 1935 Blackshirt field exercises were held across Italy involving 34 battalions, falling to 17 in 1938 before rising again to 24 in 1939, when war in Europe was looming large.

1ª Divisione Corazzata 'M' training with a German 88mm Flak 36/37 gun in the summer of 1943. Artillery crewmen, who were trained by the anti-aircraft and coastal artillery militia, were the only specialist troops at the disposal of the Blackshirts. (Archivio Centrale dello Stato, Rome)

Formal and parade drills were held in very high esteem. The Blackshirts were the first to introduce the 'Roman parade step', an imitation of the German goose-step passed off as the restoration of an old Roman tradition. To train the instructors needed for all the units and formations of the MVSN, ten courses were held in Rome with 1,280 officers attending, plus another five courses for NCOs with 930 attending. A little later the Italian version of the goose-step was introduced in almost all units and formations of the armed forces.

From the German point of view, the quality of the Blackshirts' technical training only improved following the creation of the 1ª Divisione Corazzata 'M'. The first soldier on the right is probably a German instructor for the crew of this Sturmgeschütz III Ausf. G, 12 of which were delivered to the Italians. (Archivio Centrale dello Stato, Rome)

Only from the summer of 1939 was there more adequate and methodical training for the Blackshirt divisions sent to Libya and for the legions and the battalions attached to the army infantry divisions. In Libya, this consisted of desert marches to acquaint them with the environment and climate. As a typical example, between November and December 1939 the 219ª Legione of the '23 Marzo' division held a series of exercises which included squad training in movement and combat, platoon field reconnaissance tactics, arrangement of defensive fire points (including defensive and barrage fire), setting up a counterattack and switching from march to combat deployment in difficult terrain. Such training would probably have proved adequate and useful if the Blackshirt divisions had been employed in a more suitable terrain and against a different enemy, especially given their lack of motorized transport (the '23 Marzo' only had 49 light and 35 heavy lorries) and their obsolete anti-tank weapons. When Italy entered World War II in June 1940 Marshal Italo Balbo, the commander in Libya, introduced more practical training, which followed the creation of truck-borne special companies made up of two anti-tank platoons armed with the Solothurn anti-tank rifle and one machine-gun platoon. Training would not start until July 1940, however, after delivery of the 81mm mortars from Italy. In the same month, officers were allowed to observe a field exercise that included tanks, but no actual practice with anti-tank weapons was allowed for, which were both inadequate and scarce. The suggested way to deal with tanks was by using Molotov cocktails thrown against the turrets, which were then ignited using hand grenades. This kind of action required 'men with firm hearts and bold initiative', of which there were some, but this was certainly not enough in the face of a better trained, more determined, and better armed and equipped enemy, who would eventually defeat the Blackshirt divisions.

A cheering group of Blackshirts, who have recently arrived in Ethiopia, 1935. This was an extremely popular war among the Italian people, and boosted volunteer enlistment in the Blackshirt units. (Laboratorio Storico-Iconografico della Facoltà di Scienze Politiche Università Roma Tre)

Following the limitations imposed by the Italian Army, enlistment in front-line Blackshirt units was restricted to those aged between 26 and 36. As a consequence, the men were older than the average army soldier. (Archivio Centrale dello Stato, Rome)

Training of the *legioni* attached to the army infantry divisions was also lacking, this time because of uncertainty about their use in the battlefield. Army infantry regiments were to be used as crack elements, a role which did not suit the smaller, more lightly equipped *legioni*, which were therefore employed in more 'agile' roles where they could move faster and more easily around the battlefield. Cooperation between army infantry and the Blackshirts was deemed impossible, so they had to be used in fast, opportune raids before a main attack and, following a breakthrough, in widening any breaches made in the enemy defences. In defence, they could only be used in counterattacks against targets of opportunity, and for manning the line. Clearly a degree of inter-service cooperation should have been attained for proper use of the *legioni* on the battlefield, but by spring 1940 their training only envisaged squad and firing exercises on Sundays and, if possible, following a partial mobilization, platoon and possibly company exercises. Blackshirt battalions could only undergo 20–30 days' training in the local training grounds or during army field exercises following full mobilization. Their actual mobilization started in April 1940, but only for Blackshirt battalions (without *legioni* HQs, machine-gun companies, and replacements); one month later, on the eve of war, it was clearly stated that only mobilized battalions would take part in field exercises in order to improve their technical and tactical skills. To that end, each Blackshirt could fire only up to a maximum of 12 rounds for handguns, 60 rounds for rifles, and 40 rounds for automatic rifles, while 100 rounds were available for the machine guns. The rank and file were allowed to throw two hand grenades, and 60 mortar grenades were available for training. The reality was that many Blackshirts were thrust into battle in 1940 in the Western Alps or in Greece without having fired a single shot; the XCIII Battaglione was deployed at the Greek front line after a single live-fire exercise, while many Blackshirts in the IV Battaglione had last done military service some five or six years previously. When possible, units had to be pulled from the front line to refit and retrain, but the same problems remained; in March 1941 the 80ª Legione was pulled out for further training for which only six rounds and two hand grenades were available for the rank and file, 20 rounds for the automatic rifles, and three rounds for the mortars.

There was never a shortage of officers in Blackshirt units, save for in the junior echelons. This image shows the legion commander (*console comandante*), a former *Squadrista*, wearing a war merit promotion badge and surrounded by his officers; a *seniore* right behind him and a *centurione* can be seen on the right. (Archivio Centrale dello Stato, Rome)

These deficiencies were never really made good for the average Blackshirt *legioni* and battalions, especially those that remained in the Balkans for garrison and anti-partisan duties. The exceptions were the improved and increased training courses for NCOs, especially radio operators, and the special training provided for reconnaissance platoons, which every battalion had to create from selected personnel. According to specific orders, their training ranged from individual training in the field (aimed at improving their skills in covering ground, firing their guns, and close combat) to squad and platoon reconnaissance patrols, aimed at enabling them to move unseen and approach the enemy lines either to observe or to attack small isolated groups. Special intelligence sections also had to be created by *legione* and battalion HQs, with the specific purpose of collecting and analyzing every piece of information supplied by reconnaissance patrols, which, for this very purpose, were also taught about enemy uniforms, rank insignia, and combat tactics.

It was only with the 'M' battalions, in particular the amphibious ones, that a more thorough, accurate, and specific training programme was created for the Blackshirts. From autumn 1941 (officially 1 October) these battalions gathered to train in two purpose-built field exercise camps in the suburbs of Rome. Although there were no changes to the basic training, other than including special training for heavy weapons battalions with their heavy mortars and anti-tank guns, the longer training period they were accorded plus their distinctive character as an elite force helped turn them into effective fighting units, whether employed against unfavourable odds on the Eastern Front or against the partisans in the Balkans. The amphibious 'M' battalions (*da sbarco*), formed in late 1940, were the only ones to have special training, with the invasion of Malta in mind; this comprised embarking and disembarking from barges and fishing vessels, the only kind of landing craft that was available. More specifically, given the high cliffs of the Maltese coast, special gangways were constructed, which required a certain amount of training to master.

A few words must be devoted to the training of the armoured 1ᵃ Divisione Corazzata Camicie Nere 'M', which used German armoured vehicles and weapons. Training was led at first by German specialists, and proved arduous because the Blackshirts lacked personnel who possessed even basic technical knowledge. AFV drivers and 88mm anti-aircraft gunners had to be gathered from all over Italy from every MVSN unit, and eventually it was necessary to resort to army tank drivers for a demonstration field exercise that was held on 10 July 1943 with Mussolini as a spectator. However, the German instructors advised that some time would still be needed before the unit could be combat ready. Following Mussolini's downfall two weeks later, the fact that several officers were replaced by army ones did not bring the unit anywhere close to combat readiness before Italy's surrender on 8 September 1943.

BELIEF AND BELONGING

From their inception, the *Squadristi* and their heirs the Blackshirts used violence as a means to overcome their adversaries. The *Squadre d'Azione* were modelled on the World War I *Arditi*, even in their appearance, with their black shirts, fez hats, daggers, and their identity songs. Fascism's obsession with the greatness of ancient Rome was another important influence on the Blackshirts, notably in the imagery of the bundle of fasces, the names of both units and ranks, and aspirations of future imperial might. Such characteristics became hallmarks of the Blackshirts which endured the many changes that followed, such as the transition from the *Squadre d'Azione* to the MVSN, the development of the concept of 'Fascism as a revolution' into 'Fascism as an institution' in the years following Mussolini's rise to power, and particularly the reorganization of the MVSN in the mid-1920s. Indeed, during the latter period, many of the original *Squadristi* were resentful of the rigid discipline introduced in the MVSN and the loss of the revolutionary character of early Fascism, and as a result they were now seen as more of a problem than an asset. In 1925, when Mussolini institutionalized his dictatorship, the Blackshirts simply got rid of most of the *Squadristi*; they were replaced, especially at higher levels, by monarchists, such as ex-armed forces officers.

A nice study of the sense of comradeship that existed amongst the Blackshirts. In the war against Greece the 15ᵃ Legione 'Leonessa' was attached to the Divisione 'Lupi di Toscana' (its wolf's head insignia is just visible on the chest of the Blackshirt to the right). (Piero Crociani)

Blackshirt losses

Losses suffered by Blackshirts units during World War II are hard to determine, but a few select figures may give some idea of the situation. A survey of the period 10 June 1940–31 August 1942 reported 14,900 casualties, which included 2,560 killed in action (KIA, of which 153 were officers), 10,293 wounded in action (WIA, including 273 officers) and 2,047 missing in action (MIA, including 125 officers); there were also 8,391 prisoners captured in North Africa (138 of which were officers), and all of the 26,000 Blackshirts in Italian East Africa were lost (losses there included 323 KIA, 286 WIA, and 371 MIA). North Africa alone accounted for 298 KIA, 302 WIA, and 640 MIA, while in the war against Greece Blackshirt losses were 1,362 KIA (92 officers), 3,404 WIA (185 officers), and 913 MIA (75 officers). Anti-partisan war in the Balkans had cost 417 KIA, 629 WIA, and 40 MIA up to that point. Blackshirt units on the Eastern Front had lost 121 KIA, 550 WIA and 81 MIA to date. By January–February 1943 total losses on the Eastern Front were 172 officers and 3,840 Blackshirts; only 630 of the 2,800-strong 63ª Legione 'Tagliamento' returned home, along with about 400 from the once 1,792-strong Legione 'Leonessa'.

The Blackshirts still employed the same uniforms, organization, and terminology of the early *Squadre d'Azione*, but many there were many changes too. Most of the early Blackshirts were World War I veterans (especially of the *Arditi*), ideologically nationalistic, and heavily influenced by their war-time experiences. For many of the young wartime officers, who had led men into battle and faced death, the return to former employment or study was problematic, but in the early Fascist movement they found a suitable framework which promised radical changes to the old, outdated institutions and, above all, effective opposition to their 'red' Socialist and Communist enemies. Although the birth of the MVSN seemed to promise other radical changes, such as new armed forces, little actually happened, and by 1931, less than ten years after Mussolini's rise to power, the radical ideologies would all but disappear from the ranks of the Blackshirts, together with the men who proposed them.

A statistical examination of the Blackshirts in 1931 shows that most of them came either from the most developed areas of Italy or those closely tied to the state apparatus, i.e. northern (41 per cent) and central Italy (31 per cent), while the less developed areas of southern Italy and the islands of Sicily and Sardinia only provided 28 per cent. This clearly suggests most Blackshirts at this time were not radicals. Furthermore, an examination of the age breakdown reveals that most were young men aged around 20 (23 per cent) and farmers (28 per cent), with only a limited percentage of students and professionals (nine per cent), and employees (seven per cent). Youngsters had always formed a large part of the Blackshirts from the outset; before their compulsory stint of military service, many had joined them purely in search of adventure and excitement. However, Fascist ideological indoctrination made joining the Blackshirt ranks a natural step in the education and formation of the individual for subsequent generations.

The war against Ethiopia brought (albeit short) life to Mussolini's dream of a new empire, and concluded the transformation process for the Blackshirts, notably with expansion of the combat units. The latter were still made up of a large number of veterans from World War I and the early years of Fascism, but they also drew in a large number of youngsters unrelated to either of these – half of the force that volunteered were less than 17 years old at the time of Mussolini's rise to power. Thus, while Fascist ideology still played a background role, the imprint given to the war against Ethiopia focused more on the myths of nationalism, a 'new Roman empire', and, last but not least, revenge for the defeat suffered at the hands of the Ethiopians at Adwa some

BATTAGLIONI 'M' DA SBARCO, TRAINING FOR THE ASSAULT ON MALTA, SPRING 1942

Four 'M' landing battalions were formed in 1940 and later grouped together in the Gruppo Battaglioni 'M' da sbarco; they were earmarked to take part in the planned assault on Malta – Operation *C-3* (or *Herkules*, as the Germans knew it) – although this never actually took place. During the spring of 1942 intensive training was conducted for this planned operation, which included landing in difficult terrain such as at the base of rocky cliffs. One major hurdle to overcome was the lack of suitable landing craft, and the troops were forced to use fishing boats and barges. Overall, the equipment and weaponry of the Gruppo Battaglioni da sbarco was better than average, with a greater allowance of heavy machine guns (the third man in the centre of the picture is carrying a Breda 37 8mm HMG) and 9mm Breda 30 automatic rifles (as carried over the shoulder of the fourth figure in the line). They were also amongst the first to be equipped with the new 9mm Moschetto Automatico Beretta 38 (which was in fact a machine pistol) and the distinctive 'samurai' ammunition carrier (worn by the first figure), which could accommodate up to 12 machine pistol magazines (five on the front, seven on the back) and six hand grenades in the frontal pouches. This would see greater use, though still in limited quantities, among the pro-German armed forces of the Repubblica Sociale Italiana (1943–45).

40 years previously. It is worth noting that one entire Blackshirt division, the 6ᵃ 'Tevere', was made up of expatriate students and army veterans, most of whom became Blackshirts by default.

There were of course several reasons behind any decision to join the Blackshirt combat *legioni* and battalions, including a political or ideological drive, pure opportunism, nationalism or patriotism, or just a search for adventure. The Blackshirts were the only all-volunteer Italian force in existence, and thus the only way in which volunteers could take part in the war. However, ideology came to the fore once more in Italy's involvement in the Spanish Civil War of 1936–39. The latter was markedly political, something done not just for the sake of one's own country; as the Fascist propaganda boasted, Italy's involvement in the war was to answer the 'cry of our Spanish brothers' in the fight against communism. It is revealing that in this war the overall strength of the Blackshirt combat units involved actually fell to just a quarter of that during the war against Ethiopia, despite the more favourable conditions (especially financial) that the volunteers enjoyed. Furthermore, the setbacks suffered during this war, together with the high losses, would soon lead to a certain degree of disillusionment; waging war against Ethiopia was one thing, but fighting hard against determined enemies was something else altogether.

Conditions of service

The conditions of service for the Blackshirts were not particularly attractive. The relative few on active duty received only four-fifths of the army wages, while full army wages would only be paid to all Blackshirts after mobilization. At the end of their period of service, the Blackshirts would be given a long-service medal, some form of compensatory payment, and possibly career advancement. The chief benefits of service, though, were access to a whole range of social services, which included, amongst others, summer vacations in Fascist party facilities, medical and health insurance, life insurance, and the equivalent of the army personnel's privileged retirement conditions and pension. Joining the Blackshirts appeared to be an easy commitment to make, apparently neither taking up much time nor energy, since actual mobilizations were rare and often lasted for short periods of time. The risks and discomforts were counterbalanced by aspects such as a better chance of getting a job in state or party organizations or even merely by the improved social status which service could grant. Without doubt, many of those who volunteered in 1935–36, and in the years that followed, sought such practical advantages – particularly farmers, manual workers, and the unemployed (many of whom, in the wake of the world economic crisis of 1929, were no longer allowed entry to the United States) – including a possible future in the colonies. Yet, it would be a mistake to focus exclusively on pure opportunism; in fact, most of those who settled in Italian East Africa from 1936 would join local Blackshirt battalions when Italy entered World War II, willingly giving their support to these local militia in the last stand of the doomed Italian empire.

An example of the early Blackshirt duty uniform, introduced in the early 1930s. Note the open collar and the dagger, which was later only worn by paratroopers in Libya in the 1930s. (Piero Crociani)

On the Eastern Front, in summer 1941, two Blackshirts are having their meal atop a decapitated statue of Stalin. Both here and in Yugoslavia the Blackshirts' ideological hatred of Communism played a key role. (Archivio Centrale dello Stato, Rome)

On the other hand, it is undeniable that by 1940 the Blackshirts had already discarded a good deal of their political and ideological baggage. The overall low recruitment figures, which fell below the upper ceiling imposed by the army, were in part the consequence of a sort of generation gap; only a small minority of those serving in the Blackshirt *legioni* and battalions were first-time volunteers, while the vast majority were aged around 30 and who had fought in Ethiopia and Spain, but who had not fuelled the political drive of the early years of the Fascist revolution. Propaganda, political motivation and ideology would prove inadequate in boosting their morale when they encountered dramatic setbacks both in Greece and in the Western Desert. This becomes clearer when we consider that the Fascist regime was ineffective in its use of propaganda. This was not a political or ideological war, but neither was it a nationalistic one like 1935–36 had been. The enemy was now stronger and the final outcome uncertain.

Two Blackshirts training in Italy before leaving for East Africa, 1935. Both wear the denim fatigue uniform. The one on the left wears the MVSN badge on his cap, while the other has the new badge for the Blackshirt combat units stationed in the colonies. He also wears his medal ribbons on his lapel. (Laboratorio Storico-Iconografico della Facoltà di Scienze Politiche Università Roma Tre)

As World War II developed, the Blackshirt battalions were affected by a whole series of factors that further reduced any nationalistic, political or ideological motivations they may have been driven by. The conditions of service on campaign were often appalling, caused primarily by the lack of field service units in the Blackshirt *legioni* and battalions, for which they depended on their parent army divisions. The organization of the Blackshirt medical services is a revealing example. The establishment included medical personnel mainly active in the homeland, which could also be mobilized along with Blackshirt *legioni* and battalions, at least one medical *centurione*, some junior medical officers, plus former army medical aides and orderlies. During the 1935–36 war against Ethiopia, the Blackshirt divisions had a medical section with an HQ (one medical *seniore*, a chaplain, two NCOs, 11 Blackshirts, and four drivers with an ambulance), a horse-borne medical unit with two officers, two NCOs and 25 Blackshirts, a mule train with one NCO and 30 Blackshirts with as many mules, and a two-section stretcher bearer unit with one officer, two NCOs, 158 Blackshirts, and 18 mules.

A fine study of a *centurione* of the Gruppo Montagna, the first to arrive in Eritrea. He is wearing the Alpine hat (for use in Italy) that displays his rank insignia, the latter also being worn on his shoulder straps. (Laboratorio Storico-Iconografico della Facoltà di Scienze Politiche Università Roma Tre)

They would look after medical supplies, provide first aid, collect wounded and sick Blackshirts from the front line, and send them back to the army field hospitals. First aid at the front line was dealt with by the two medical officers, one aide and two orderlies assigned to each battalion. The situation did not improve in 1940, with each *legione* having one medical *centurione* and one aide in its HQ, plus one junior medical officer, one aide and two orderlies in each battalion (it is worth pointing out that a *legione* was 1,400 strong). At the front a dressing station was established to take care of the lightly wounded who, once treated, were sent back to their unit; those no longer deemed fit for front line duty were dealt with as well, but were then sent back to the army field hospitals. The medical experiences of those deployed in Greece and Albania were appalling; the harsh climate and unpaved mountain roads often required the wounded to be carried either on stretchers or by mule, often on journeys that lasted for hours. The situation improved for those on the Eastern Front, climate apart, and in the Balkans, where motor vehicles were more widely available.

Two factors would steer the Blackshirts back to their political and ideological origins: the development of a political, anti-communist struggle which was started by the German attack on the Soviet Union and the decision to create the elite 'M' battalions. Involvement in the war against the Soviet Union and against the partisans in Yugoslavia gave a vital boost to both the morale and the ideological convictions of the Blackshirts, whose political identity was rapidly fading. This time, however, the Fascist propaganda supporting the recent involvement would concentrate on a few, select units that offered greater political reliability; these included both the *Squadristi Battaglioni*, formed from the veterans of the early years of the Fascist revolution and deployed in Yugoslavia, and the 'M' battalions. Built around selected cadres of skilled and reliable officers and NCOs, the latter would include the newly drafted young Blackshirts born in 1923–24 – those who had grown up in Mussolini's Fascist Italy and, as such, were highly motivated and politically inclined to believe that to fight for the cause of the Fascist revolution in such units was the highest honour they could dream of. In the case of the 'M' battalions, Fascism took a further step forward by adding to its core ideological themes of the proletarian struggle against Bolshevism and Freemasonry certain even more radical themes that were borrowed from the Waffen-SS (albeit without much success).

A group of Blackshirt officers in Ethiopia, 1936. The variety of uniforms, which was common among rearguard units (this photo was taken at a field hospital), is remarkable; note the cummerbunds; the second man from the left has a red cross on his chest, denoting his status as a chaplain. (Laboratorio Storico-Iconografico della Facoltà di Scienze Politiche Università Roma Tre)

Although the 'M' battalions would bear the brunt of the defeats on the Eastern Front and in the anti-partisan war in the Balkans, by 1943 they still ranked as an elite with a strong political and ideological background and, as such, posed the greatest danger to any attempt to bring about change in the Italian regime. The VIII and XXIX 'M' battalions were recalled from the Balkans to take part in the parade celebrating the anniversary of 1 February 1943 (both with two-thirds of their established strength), but were sent back as early as the 16th. Later on, the army would be greatly concerned about the presence of the 1ª Divisione Corazzata Camicie Nere 'M', which should have been redeployed away from Rome. Such concerns would prove to be exaggerated, as proved by the lack of Blackshirt reaction to Mussolini's downfall on 25 July 1943. Certainly at this stage of the war the average Blackshirt no longer cared for Il Duce or Fascism, while the elite 'M' units either lacked the opportunity (being posted in remote areas) or, as in the case of the 1ª Divisione, simply suffered from being a mixture of army personnel and Blackshirts. A few months later, the core members of the 'M' battalions would have no such doubts, when they joined the Germans to continue the fight.

A Blackshirt of the 49ª Legione 'San Marco' from Venice in the Balkans, 1942. He is wearing the 1940 model grey-green uniform, but little other equipment – not even the ammunition pouches for his Moschetto 91 rifle. (Archivio Centrale dello Stato, Rome)

Blackshirts of the 112ª Legione disembarking at Durazzo (Durres) in Albania, January 1941. They are wearing the model 1934 greatcoat and a mixture of puttees and grey knee socks. Many other units hurriedly sent to Albania lacked even this basic protective gear. (Archivio Centrale dello Stato, Rome)

APPEARANCE AND EQUIPMENT

The Blackshirt uniform introduced in 1923 was innovative. The jacket and trousers were grey-green in colour (in common with the army), though the jacket introduced for the first time the open collar, later to be adopted by the armed forces as well. However, the similarities ended there; they wore a black shirt (inherited from the *Squadristi*) with a black tie, which closely linked them to the Fascist party and its early origins. Likewise, lapel badges (known as flames) were black and shaped like the infantry ones, themselves inherited from World War I *Arditi*, while the star (common to all the members of the armed forces) was replaced by the Fascist bundle of fasces (*il fascio*) in metal. Headgear included a grey-green *Alpino* (mountain troop)-style hat for officers and the black fez, inherited again from the *Arditi*, for other ranks. Headgear insignia, other than for generals (who sported an eagle holding a bundle of fasces) was simple, comprising a bundle of fasces with a roundel at the bottom, where the number of the *legione* was indicated. Blackshirt combat units would later introduce some changes which included a wreath of laurels surrounding the *fascio*, with a roundel at the bottom and the house of Savoy star, denoting subordination to the king, at the top. (In 1935–36 the flames were worn with simpler insignia introduced for Blackshirt units serving in the colonies; these had two crossed swords for combat Blackshirts with, in 1940, the light infantry's cornet superimposed.) Variations included an Aesculapian snake for medical officers and a Latin cross for chaplains, always superimposed on the *fascio*.

Rank insignia for the common soldier also had its distinctive peculiarities; given their status as a semi-permanent force, the Blackshirts only adopted a limited number of ranks, which were eventually increased in February 1936 during the war against Ethiopia, with these ranks becoming permanent in July. Peacetime ranks only included basic ones equivalent to private (*camicia nera*), sergeant (*capo squadra*), and officers (without the equivalent of lieutenant-

BELOW LEFT
Yugoslavia, summer 1942; Capo Manipolo Walter Crociani (author's father) wearing the distinctive black shirt with the lapels overlapping those of his *sahariana* jacket. Note the 'M' fasces and the insignia of university militia worn on the chest. (Piero Crociani)

BELOW RIGHT
A *console* monitoring the tactical situation in Albania, 1941. Note the *Ardito* badge on his arm, two war merit promotion badges on his chest, and the red ribbons worn on the cuffs (matched by the red *fasci*) denoting his former role as a *Squadrista*. (Archivio Centrale dello Stato, Rome)

Vice Capo Squadra Achille Nunziati at Martuba, March 1940 (first on the right). Note how all the other three men are wearing the grey-green European Model 1940 uniforms with sweaters over their black shirts. (Bruno Nunziati)

colonel); from 1936 six new ranks were introduced for enlisted men, NCOs and warrant officers (the Italian *maresciallo*), plus four others for officers. These included the ranks of *primo capo manipolo* (senior lieutenant) and *primo centurione* (senior captain), reserved to those who (with 12 years of seniority) surrendered the ranks formerly held to enlist voluntarily. Officer candidates held the rank of *aspirante sotto capo manipolo*, and the special rank of *aiutante di battaglia* (aide), not part of the formal hierarchy, was granted to those who had distinguished themselves in battle. Blackshirt honorary ranks also included those of *caporale* and *primo caporale d'onore* (corporal and honorary lance corporal); the first was awarded to Hitler and the second to Mussolini. The rank insignia would be changed several times. At first it was made up of simple stripes (with chevron-style stripes worn on the headgear), then, from the early 1930s, it consisted of stripes with a lozenge on top, worn in the Italian Air Force style on both forearms. Only in 1938 was army-style rank insignia introduced for corporals and NCOs, worn on the upper arm, the only difference being the colours used: red for corporals (for the army, black), silver for NCOs (for the army, yellow). The warrant officer equivalent *aiutanti* wore rank insignia on the shoulder straps.

The semi-permanent character of the Blackshirts units, their own attitudes, and the political background contributed to some peculiarities in their dress and appearance. Their uniforms included still widely used grey-green puttees, worn with leather boots which, at first, the Blackshirts had to buy themselves, contributing to an early mixture of colours and styles worn. Winter clothing only specified a grey-green cape, while summer uniform was something of a major innovation for the otherwise conservative Italian armed forces; the Blackshirts would remain in shirtsleeves order, using only a sort of cummerbund, an extremely unusual idea for the time.

Other differences did exist between the Blackshirts and the armed forces, closely denoting their purported special status as a 'Fascist army'; when passed in review, the Blackshirts would not present arms, but rather thrust their right arms outwards holding their daggers, a characteristic and irreplaceable item inherited, once again, from the *Arditi*. Also, the Blackshirts did not use the formal military salute, but instead employed the Fascist (or 'Roman', in the official terminology) one, with

A Blackshirt on sentry duty in the Balkans. The lack of suitable winter clothing afflicted many Blackshirt units, the only exceptions being the 'M' battalions sent to the Eastern Front. (Archivio Centrale dello Stato, Rome)

the right arm and hand raised high. Officer uniform differed only slightly from that of other ranks in the early years, in an attempt to denote the proletarian nature of the Blackshirts; they wore riding boots (again, privately bought), had double black stripes along their trousers, and in wintertime were allowed to wear the army grey-green greatcoat. Needless to say, the expansion of the MVSN and the Blackshirt units in the 1930s produced a certain degree of embellishment in terms of their uniforms; officers were proscribed black evening dress and white summer dress, worn with a characteristic hard fez hat. The shape of the fez also changed for the Blackshirts, to whom a winter greatcoat was also supplied. Service uniforms became more similar to those used by the army (which in 1934 introduced the open collar jacket) down to the introduction of the forage or side cap, with rank insignia worn on the left side, and the peaked cap.

Combat dress differed little from service dress save for a few details. In 1935, following the mass mobilization for the war against Ethiopia, an extraordinary effort was made to supply the army and the Blackshirts with comfortable uniforms and modern equipment. A new tropical khaki uniform made of light cotton and cut in the shape of the one worn in Europe was introduced in 1935; at first it featured the distinctive inverted V-shaped cuffs, and was only distributed to Blackshirt units when they began to embark for Africa. The most interesting items issued were the ankle boots, which prevented the soldiers from using puttees (still worn with breeches), a welcome innovation. The uniforms and equipment of the Blackshirts in East Africa were the same of those used by the army. The black shirt, which was impractical in this climate, was replaced by the khaki one, but a special version for the Blackshirts with black shoulder straps, and worn with a black tie, was widely used. Thus, insignia was the sole distinctive feature. This included the lapel badges with *fascio* and divisional badges in the shape of a shield, similar to those used by the army, bearing a Roman eagle with a *fascio* and the name of the division. Steel helmets were not used in this theatre, but were part of the issued equipment; Blackshirts still wore the World War I, French-style 'Adrian' model. Widespread use was made of tropical hats or topees, made of cork, which were very comfortable. Officers used to place an Italian green–white–red cockade below the insignia on them. Another distinctive feature for officers was the use of riding boots or leggings. A few changes apart, like the new-

GRUPPO BATTAGLIONI 'M' 'LEONESSA', EASTERN FRONT, SUMMER 1942
Eleven out of the 22 'M' battalions were deployed on the Eastern Front; as for the rest, six were deployed in Yugoslavia, four comprised the landing battalions, and one was deployed in Tunisia. This balance clearly shows how important the war against the Soviet Union was for Mussolini. The first to be sent was the 63ª Legione (LXIII and LXXIX battalions) in June 1941, along with the Corpo di Spedizione Italiano in Russia (CSIR, Italian Expeditionary Corps in Russia), eventually renamed Gruppo Battaglioni Camicie Nere 'M' 'Tagliamento'. Along with the Gruppo Battaglioni Camicie Nere 'M' 'Montebello' (VI, XXX, XII) this unit formed the Raggruppamento Camicie Nere '3 Gennaio', which was deployed on the Eastern Front in summer 1942 along with the Raggruppamento Camicie Nere '23 Marzo' (Gruppo Battaglioni Camicie Nere 'M' 'Leonessa', with XIV, XV, XXXVIII; and 'Valle Scrivia', with V, XXXIV, XLI). Training, weapons and equipment were improved, and these were also the only Blackshirt units to have a degree of motorization. Here we see a group of Blackshirts of the 'Leonessa' checking captured Soviet weapons (including a 14.5mm PTRD model 1941 anti-tank rifle and the ubiquitous 7.62mm PPSh model 1941 MP) while a medical officer is attending to the arm of a wounded comrade. Medical officers had lapel badges and rank insignia lined with red (in July 1943 new lapel badges were issued with a rectangular red backing), and had a special cap badge. Lacking many service units, the Blackshirts (like their army equivalents) only dealt with the lightly wounded, while serious wounds and injuries had to be treated by the divisional or corps army medical units.

ABOVE LEFT

Two portraits of a Blackshirt of the 'M' Battaglione 'IX Settembre' in Abruzzo, winter 1943. This unit was formed after the Italian surrender from elements of the L and XLII 'M' amphibious battalions. Pieces of equipment like the 'samurai' corset shown here would be retained. (Archivio Centrale dello Stato, Rome)

ABOVE RIGHT

A mixed group of Waffen-SS troops and Blackshirts, who formed part of Mussolini's bodyguard, pose for a photo in Maderno, Lake Garda, in 1944. (Count Ernesto G. Vitetti)

style jacket introduced in 1940 (without shaped cuffs), the same style and type of tropical uniform was still used in 1940 both in Italian East Africa and in Libya, though with puttees. In Libya the Blackshirts were at first issued the grey-green European uniform worn with the topee; the tropical one was only issued in late 1940, but even then the European grey-green overcoat was still in wide use.

The equipment used during the 1935–36 war remained in use until 1943. The basic webbing for the rank and file comprised a leather belt hooked to a leather strap that was looped around the neck – barely adequate for supporting the weight of the two rifle cartridge pouches worn on the front. The bayonet, with frog and scabbard, was the only other item to be attached to the belt, along with the Blackshirt dagger and scabbard, which was always worn on the left side. All other pieces of equipment were worn with their own strapping, which created problems when those carrying all their equipment wanted to remove it quickly; the relevant items included the gas mask (the new model 1935 carried in the characteristic tube-shaped bag), bread bag and canteen, plus the model 1939 knapsack, often carried with the rolled-up blanket below and the camouflaged tent quarter on the upper side. There were different varieties of entrenching tool, but these were not always available to the troops. The only changes to this somewhat basic equipment were for those Blackshirts armed with the Breda 30 automatic rifle; they wore only the belt with the automatic rifle kit and a pistol holster. Officers had a better, more robust belt with a single strap used to carry the pistol holster and the dagger; other pieces of standard equipment were the map and the binocular cases. Following the adoption of the Beretta model 38 machine pistol, different magazine pouches came into use; the most widespread one, which matched the style and shape of the German MP pouch, was made of cloth, save for the leather top flaps. Amphibious Blackshirt battalions were also supplied with variants of the 'samurai' corset, with pouches for ammunition clips and magazines plus hand grenades.

The deficiencies in the area of personal equipment were matched by those of the field uniform issued in Europe from 1940; it was both impractical and uncomfortable. The grey-green uniform was often made of synthetic fibres, due to the shortage of wool; the tunic had an open collar and four pockets; early versions also had a cloth belt. The trousers were once again worn with puttees, though from the mid 1930s many Blackshirts would replace them with

The Legione 'M' Guardia del Duce, Mussolini's bodyguard in the RSI, was one of the few 'M' Blackshirt battalions to be newly raised after 1943. Some of the men are wearing the 'M' with *fascio* on their collarless (paratrooper style) *sahariana* jackets. (Count Ernesto G. Vitetti)

long, elasticated black socks that were rolled up and worn with short white wool socks on top of them. Apart from the overcoat, which proved inadequate in winter conditions during the war against Greece, the only cold-weather clothing available to the Blackshirts was the sheepskin sleeveless jacket; this could be purchased locally on the personal initiative of the commanders, and was issued to the units deployed on the Eastern Front. It was intended that officers should wear the same uniform as the other Blackshirts, though the use of various privately purchased items, the service trousers with their black stripes, and riding boots was quite common. The only characteristic feature of the Blackshirts in Europe, apart from their dagger, was their insignia; besides rank insignia, this included the painted badge worn on the model 1933 steel helmet, headgear insignia, and the wartime black lapel badges (which were shorter than the peacetime ones) with the metal *fascio* or, for the 'M' battalions, the *fascio* intertwined with the red 'M' for Mussolini. These would have been the only ones to receive a large number of special uniforms, which included the denim fatigue dress worn during training and the blue overalls worn by the tank crews of the 1ª Divisione Corazzata.

Blackshirt officers would wear privately purchased clothes whenever possible, like the one on the left here, who is sporting a non-regulation overcoat. (Archivio Centrale dello Stato, Rome)

The fez was the issued headgear for the Blackshirt rank and file, while officers and NCOs wore either sidecaps or field peaked caps with their rank insignia on the side (for a short period, a black sidecap was also in use). Former members of the *Squadre d'Azione* had special insignia, which included a red enamelled *fascio* and a red stripe on the cuffs – the red symbolizing the blood shed during the Fascist revolution. Following Mussolini's downfall on 25 July 1943 the black shirt (which had already been replaced in many instances with the grey-green one) and all the *fasci* disappeared, the latter being replaced by the armed forces' stars.

THE EXPERIENCE OF BATTLE

The Blackshirts' experiences of battle covered a wide timeframe and different theatres of operations. One challenge is the fragmented perspective that results from this, while another is the fact that many who served were reluctant to recall their past experiences or record their individual memories in written sources in the wake of the discrediting of Fascism. Blackshirt memoirs are thus scarce and not always reliable; those dating back to the pre-World War II period were heavily influenced by Fascist propaganda and its mythology, while post-war ones were largely produced in the context of its downfall. Yet, there are some good accounts available, particularly for the 1935–36 war against Ethiopia. The latter was a popular cause, seen as befitting Italy and in general as a kind of adventure. It involved some hard fighting, and was also a war fought by the Blackshirts in the spirit of their early struggles in Italy before Mussolini's rise to power. Things took on quite a different shape during the Spanish Civil War, when the grim faces of death, fear, and hardship were everywhere to be seen in a country in ruins. Needless to say this represented a key moment of disillusionment for many Blackshirts, who were compelled to face up to how different the reality of war was from the image put forward by Fascist propaganda.

The influence of the events in Spain on Blackshirt attitudes before the outbreak of World War II is hard to discern. It is also hard to make general statements about whether the Blackshirts were mere opportunists or whether they were prime, highly enthusiastic supporters of Mussolini's desire for war. These two views might indeed happily coexist, as some Blackshirts are known to have volunteered with the thought in mind that being in 'Mussolini's army' could be a good way to avoid many of the dangers and discomforts of the war; however, it fails to explain why in 1940 the Blackshirts' strength was at an all time low. Since full mobilization of the Blackshirts only began following the outbreak of the war against Greece, and given the nature of their involvement, it is hard to separate out any pre- and post-war disillusionment felt by the soldiers. The war against Greece was, like Spain, a very hard campaign, where, once again, facing a determined enemy in heavy fighting, the harshness of climate and the full horrors of war would take their toll. A further complication is that it is hard to tell why some Blackshirt battalions performed poorly while others distinguished themselves. This genesis of the 'M' battalions marks a definitive change. The 'average' Blackshirt battalions seemed to disappear into obscurity at this stage, as if swallowed by this war that many fought with little enthusiasm. The new, elite 'M' battalions, in contrast, took centre stage, and eventually came to be exclusively identified with the Blackshirts themselves.

G

1ª DIVISIONE CORAZZATA 'M', ROME, SUMMER 1943
After the defeats at Stalingrad and in Tunisia, Hitler became concerned that Mussolini's rule might be threatened from elements within Italy. He decided to provide the Italian Army with tanks, self-propelled guns and anti-aircraft 88mm guns, which were handed over to the *milizia* through Himmler. These weapons were used to build the 1ª Divisione Corazzata Camicie Nere 'M', formed on 25 June 1943 at Chiusi from the remnants of the *legioni* once deployed on the Eastern Front. A special insignia was created for this armoured division, which can be seen on the turret skirts of this Panzer III 75mm short-barrelled M variant, though it was mainly used to cover the existing German crosses. Here a *primo capo squadra* (lance sergeant, left) shares a joke with a *centurione* (captain, centre), while other Blackshirts (who are part of the crew) look on. They are wearing variations of the tank crewman overalls first introduced in 1941, and the characteristic fez. The officer is wearing a *camiciotto sahariano* (a *sahariana*-style open shirt) and non-regulation tropical trousers. The most peculiar feature of the Divisione Corazzata 'M' was that, in spite of its intended role as Mussolini's bodyguard, it did not react to the coup against Mussolini on 25 July 1943.

Blackshirts attacking a Russian farm under the cover of a 6.5mm Breda 30. The Blackshirt on the right is carrying the ammunition case and two spare barrels for the gun on his back. (Archivio Centrale dello Stato, Rome)

It is not by chance that the most prolific series of accounts of Blackshirts stem from the units on the Eastern Front. The war against the communist Soviet Union was seen as a mission, and not merely some form of adventure. This ideological struggle helped the soldiers overcome the very difficult conditions that they would find there, but more importantly they were provided with adequate weapons and equipment to fight the enemy. Thus the harsh climate of the Russian winter, the hard fighting against a superior enemy, and the heavy losses incurred generated little resentment among those who fought there, and instead were seen and portrayed as deeds of valour and meaning in an epic struggle. This was not true for the more subtle conflict fought in the Balkans against the partisans, though. Here, the experience of battle, consisting of mopping-up operations, reprisals, and sometimes executions, seems largely to have been forgotten or at best is only whispered about. And yet this war, like the one the Blackshirts fought on the Eastern Front, seems to have marked the high point of their combat efficiency. Many veterans would say they fought against the partisans 'just as the Germans did', a claim also shared by the elite 'M' Blackshirt battalions fighting on the Eastern Front. However, we must remember that in post-war and post-Fascist Italy little credit or respect was given to this.

Disillusionment again characterized the months that lapsed between the defeats of winter 1942–43 and Mussolini's downfall on 25 July 1943. The Blackshirt legions in Sicily simply melted away in front of the Allies (like many army units), and the lack of any reaction from the Divisione Corazzata 'M' to Mussolini's downfall would suggest that the Blackshirts, like all the other Italian soldiers, were just tired of the war. The fact that only a part of them, most notably the 'M' battalions, joined the Germans after the Italian surrender on 8 September 1943 seems to prove that. The experiences of the Blackshirts in the years 1943–45 represents a kind of a watershed in their history. The sheer volume of memoirs and literature available on the period is much greater than that of the previous 20 years, which in a way generated a bizarre reaction; the previous experiences were almost forgotten while Fascism and its Blackshirt army became almost exclusively identified with the experiences of the doomed,

Blackshirts under review by an *Alpini* officer somewhere on the Eastern Front, summer 1942. Many are in shirtsleeve order, an unusual occurrence for Italian armed forces personnel. (Piero Crociani)

German-controlled Repubblica Sociale Italiana. Those who joined either the Germans or the RSI came to be labelled as true, motivated Fascists, the same ones who used to fight 'just like the Germans' and who now continued to do it under their command, but this time against the Italian partisans. The harshness of the civil war raging in Italy in this period is hard to describe, but the reflections of Carlo Mazzantini (a veteran of the Legione 'Tagliamento' who volunteered at 16) express some of the confusion and bitterness that still lingers to this day. Referring to the murder of two Blackshirt Eastern Front veterans at the hands of partisans in Italy, he commented bitterly that this was a poor reward they had been given after valiantly serving their country overseas. Having survived the experience of war in Russia, they ended up being killed 'in one of the streets of one of those cities from whence they had departed feted by songs and flags, girls and flowers'.

Blackshirts marching on the Eastern Front. In the foreground is a Breda 37 heavy machine-gun team. (Archivio Centrale dello Stato, Rome)

It would be too easy to draw a line between two different experiences of battle, one made up of expediency and disillusionment and one of a deep ideological belief and the will to fight to the last. However, a single example may help us to understand how complex the reality was. At 16, the young Blackshirt Achille Nunziati took part in the 1922 Fascist march on Rome, and in April 1923 he joined the 71ª Legione. He served in the army between 1926 and 1927, and was drafted again in the Blackshirt LXXI Battaglione in August 1939. Sent to Libya, he was promoted to *vice capo squadra* in February 1940, detached to the 181ª Legione and sent back to Italy following its disbandment in May. Demobilized between August and December 1940, he was sent back to the LXXI 'M' Battaglione and eventually posted to Yugoslavia in June 1942, where his experiences of the bloody anti-partisan war can best be described as shocking. Disarmed by the Germans after the 8 September 1943 Italian surrender, he chose internment in Germany rather than to continue fighting with them – a choice for which there was a simple explanation: he just could not bring himself to fight for Hitler and Germany. It was a choice that would place him and his family in limbo, still hated by the communists and yet seen as a traitor by many Fascists. Having returned to Italy after the end of the war, he was rescued from any partisan reprisals thanks to his brother in law, who was himself a Communist, though he remained a self-proclaimed Fascist until the very end of his life. The subsequent recognition of Achille Nunziati's experiences clearly illustrates how extremely complicated the situation became; he was acknowledged as one of the earliest Fascists by the Blackshirt veterans association, but at the same time the Italian government also acknowledged him as a resistance fighter against the post-September 1943 German occupation.

An *Alpini* colonel, probably a Fascist party official, dishing out wine to a group of Blackshirts, who seem to be wearing a variant of the *Ardito* badge on their chests. (Archivio Centrale dello Stato, Rome)

THE FINAL YEARS: 1943–45

At the same time as four of the *legioni* (17ᵃ, 95ᵃ, 171ᵃ and 173ᵃ) were opposing the Allied landings in Sicily, on 25 July 1943 Mussolini was overthrown and arrested. The only reaction from the Blackshirts came the next day, when the XVI 'M' Battaglione, recently redeployed near Rome from Yugoslavia, made a move on the capital before being halted. The Blackshirts practically ceased to exist a day or two later with a simple stroke of pen; the army took command of the units by putting one of its generals in charge, and the Blackshirts were renamed as *legionari* (legionaries). In a matter of days thousands of them (mostly officers) were replaced, while the Divisione Corazzata 'M' became an army armoured division ('Centauro'); again most of the Blackshirt officers were replaced with army ones.

The Italian surrender on 8 September 1943 marked the beginning of a new phase for the Blackshirts, which would deeply affect their future image. Following the German reaction and the disbandment of the Italian armed forces, the Blackshirt units responded in different ways. In Italy a large number of those in the former Divisione Corazzata 'M' joined the Germans to continue the fight against the Allies; the LXIII 'M' Battaglione, along with remnants from the Gruppo Battaglioni 'Tagliamento' and most of the XVI 'M' Battaglione, created the 1ᵃ Legione 'M' d'assalto 'Tagliamento', which was employed in central and northern Italy against the partisans. While the bulk of the Gruppo 'Leonessa' was moved to the north to be reorganized as an armoured unit, cadres from the XXX 'M' Battaglione, along with remnants from the Gruppo 'Montebello', created the 115ᵃ 'M' Battaglione 'Montebello' in November in northern Italy. The other large group of Blackshirts to join the Germans in Italy were the territorial legions on the eastern border, turned into the Milizia Difesa Territoriale (Territorial Defence Militia). In November the newborn Repubblica Sociale Italiana, headed by Mussolini after his rescue by German paratroopers from the Gran Sasso mountain, would bring radical changes to the former MVSN; it would be merged, along with the Carabinieri military police, into the new Guardia Nazionale Repubblicana, which would only partly keep the old

H

BLACKSHIRT, 'IX SETTEMBRE' BATTALION, NORTHERN ITALY, SUMMER 1944
Like many other units of the armed forces of the RSI, the 'M' Battaglione 'IX Settembre' was formed out of other units. Following the Italian surrender on 8 September 1943, some 300 men, including the 3rd Company of the Battaglione da sbarco 'M' L, led by Centurione Alberto Zardo, together with men from Battaglione 'M' XLII, joined up with German troops in Toulon, France. The rest were disarmed and sent to Germany as POWs. The unit, which officially took the name of Battaglione 'IX Settembre' (to mark the decision to react against the surrender of the previous day) a few months later, was attached to the German 2nd 'Brandenburg' Regiment. It returned to Italy in early October 1943, and fought partisan troops along the Adriatic coast until the summer of 1944, when it was sent to the western Alps and subsequently (in November) to eastern Prussia following the creation of the German 'Brandenburg' Division. The 200 or so men that survived were sent back to Italy in February 1945; deployed in the Venice area, most of them were executed by partisans following the May 1945 surrender.

The Blackshirt shown here **(A)** is manning a roadblock in northern Italy in summer 1944. He sports a mixture of German and Italian clothing and weaponry. He is wearing a German field cap, an Italian jacket with the distinctive Battaglione 'IX Settembre' badge **(4)** worn between the second and third button, and locally-made Italian camouflage trousers. He is armed with a Beretta 38 MP (with the new Italian made magazine holder) and a German model 24 hand grenade, but retains the MVSN dagger. Like the other members of his unit, he has retained his 'M' lapel badges, rather than adopting the new badges in use by other 'M' battalions that became part of the newly formed Guardia Nazionale Repubblicana **(3)**. Note that the 'Leonessa' battalion **(1)** was reorganized as an armoured one. A separate GNR unit, the 1ᵃ Divisione Guardia Nazionale Repubblicana 'Etna' **(2)**, was formed in Brescia in August 1944; the motto on its badge reads 'In fire I am tempered'.

1

2

A

3

4

ABOVE LEFT
At the end of April 1941 the newly formed Gruppo Battaglioni CCNN da sbarco saw its first employment, in the seizure of the Greek Ionian islands shortly after the end of the campaign. (Piero Crociani)

ABOVE RIGHT
Paying a visit to the *covo* (den), the place in Milan where Fascism was born, was a must for the Blackshirts, including these 'M' ones. (Laboratorio Storico-Iconografico della Facoltà di Scienze Politiche Università Roma Tre)

Blackshirt traditions alive. Other Blackshirt units fought against the Germans, and the remnants of the MVSN in Allied-occupied territories were eventually disbanded in November 1943.

A new territorial organization was created, along with a few new battalions that included the Legione 'M' Guardia del Duce (first formed as the LXXXII Battaglione in Forlì, close to Mussolini's birthplace, before being transformed into his bodyguard – the only newly formed unit to be named 'M'), and at least three provisional battalions: a 'parachute' one 'Mazzarini', the 'Pontida', and the 'Borg Pisani' (named after the Maltese Carmelo Borg Pisani, who joined the Blackshirts; he was later sent back to Malta and hanged for betrayal). Only a few units under German control would return to Italy from abroad; these included the 'M' Battaglione 'IX Settembre', formed from elements of L and XLII 'M' amphibious battalions and attached to II. Bataillon of the German 3. 'Brandenburg' Regiment, the XL (disbanded in summer 1944) and XXIX 'M' battaglioni from Albania and the remnants of the 107ᵃ Legione (formed in 1943), which created the Battaglione 'Venezia Giulia'. Practically all of them fought against the partisans under permanent German control, which led to progressive depletion; for example, in the summer of 1944 the Legione 'Tagliamento' was reduced down into the LXIII 'M' Battaglione. Between late 1944 and early 1945 most of these battalions would be used (along with anti-aircraft units) to create the 'Etna' division, which was actually more of a paper organization; the subordination to German command for operational matters remained in place.

The situation in the Balkans was different, though the fate of the Blackshirt battalions remained the same. At the time of Italy's surrender those stationed in Yugoslavia, Greece, and Albania had one of two choices: either join the Germans or became their prisoners. Going over to the partisans was not an option, given their ideological differences (although some in the Italian armed forces did join them). Some, such as Achille Nunziati, became prisoners, but many also opted to join the Germans. These included two legions, the 89ᵃ and 107ᵃ, and some ten battalions (XXXIII, XL, XLIX, LXXII, LXXXI 'M', LXXXII, LXXXVI, XCIV, CXLIV, and possibly the CLXII) deployed in Montenegro; XXIX 'M' Battaglione and the 92ᵃ Legione also joined the Germans in Albania like practically all the Blackshirt battalions in Greece (including XIX, XXIII, XXVIII, and XXXVI), Crete (CXLI), and the Aegean (24ᵃ Legione in Rhodes). Only a few would be sent back to Italy, which included the 107ᵃ Legione, XL, and XXIX 'M' battaglioni, some would be sent to Germany either to create the bulk of the future Italian SS Brigade (89ᵃ

Legione, XIX Battaglione) or to the divisions of the newborn army of Mussolini's RSI (XXXVI Battaglione from Greece). Most would simply remain in the area under German control, following their ups and downs. In Greece the battalions on Crete and in the Aegean remained there until the end of the war, while others formed a new *legione* ('San Marco' with the XXIII and XXVIII battaglioni) that, like other units, saw employment as a police force and in anti-partisan warfare. By the end of 1944 they pulled out from Greece following the German withdrawal, joining those already in Yugoslavia. Here, two battalions had been disbanded in the summer (XXXIIII and CXLIV), while apparently the Legione 'San Marco' was merged with the 49ª. Lacking communication with their homeland, gradual depletion awaited those units already engaged in very difficult conditions. By late summer 1944 eight battalions had already lost half of their strength. Very few of those Blackshirts would make it back to Italy after the end of the war.

Similar circumstances were experienced by those serving in Italy, though the conditions of service here were actually better than those in the Balkans, where the scarcity of German supplies meant the Blackshirts were deprived of practically everything, from uniforms to weapons, leaving them in most cases with just what they had at the time of Italy's surrender. In contrast, replacements and new provisions were available to the units serving under German control in Italy, and even to the newly formed ones; this was actually a consequence of a fall in the manpower figures, enabling the Blackshirts there to be equipped with new uniforms, sometimes also with German items, and new weapons including the once rare Beretta 38 machine pistol, now apparently in widespread use (German weapons were supplied too). New recruits were scarce, though; youngsters could freely join up, but with Italy now a manpower pool for both the Germans and the newly-formed armed forces of the RSI, every man, either a volunteer or enlisted, was jealously fought over. Many of these would eventually join the Guardia Nazionale Repubblicana and be used to create the units of the Guardia Giovanile Repubblicana (Young Republican Guard). Old Blackshirt battalions, the 'M' ones in particular, had very few recruits, since the Germans were dealing with experienced personnel, for whom no further training was required.

The differences between the Blackshirt 'old guard' and the new levy of the Guardia Nazionale Repubblicana, and of the Repubblica Sociale Italiana as a whole, are worth exploring. Not only would most of the former (mostly 'M' battalions) continue to fight under German control, often under direct German command, but they would also retain and proudly display the symbols

A group of Blackshirts photographed in 1935, shortly before the war against Ethiopia. The tropical uniforms, new rank insignia and divisional arm shields can be clearly seen. (Piero Crociani)

denoting their sense of belonging to a combat elite. No matter what uniform they wore, they retained the red 'M' with *fascio*, which identified them as the sole fighting elite of the Blackshirt combat units. The fact that these were retained even after their formal absorption into the 'Etna' division (part of the GNR), when the GNR's new lapel badges had to be worn leaving only small breast badges with the 'M' and the *fascio*, clearly demonstrates how at the end the sense of belonging would matter more than anything else. Fascist ideology was still their main motivator, something clearly demonstrated by the savage nature of their struggle against the Italian partisans, but they were also guided by a sense of continuity, and the desire to bring Italy back to the role and status she had lost. In this sense, the Blackshirt battalions were something of a peculiarity within the RSI. When, in the summer of 1944, the Fascist party created the 'black brigades' from the ranks of its members, there was no attempt to try to merge these new *Squadre d'Azione* with the GNR and the Blackshirts. Fascism had looped back to its origins just before the final showdown, but the combat elite of the 'M' battalions were still aware of who they were and were ready to fight the last battles. These took place as the Axis forces retreated northwards through Italy between late 1944 and 1945 before General Heinrich von Vietinghoff surrendered all Axis forces in Italy on 29 April 1945.

The 'Tevere' (Tiber) Blackshirt Division on parade in Italian Somaliland, 1936. The division featured a large percentage of repatriated emigrants, who were used to form the 218ª Legione Fasci Italiani all'Estero (Italian Fascists abroad). (Piero Crociani)

GLOSSARY

Alpino (pl. *Alpini*) Mountain infantry.

Ardito (pl. *Arditi*) World War I assault troops.

Armi d'accompagnamento Support weapons.

Banderas Blackshirt battalions in Spain.

Battaglione 'M' Elite battalion, formed on 1 October 1941.

Camicia Nera (pl. *Camicie Nere*, CCNN) Blackshirt.

Centuria Early sub-unit of the *legione*, equivalent to a company.

Comando Generale della MVSN MVSN's general staff

Complementi Replacements.

Coorte Early sub-unit of the *legione*, equivalent to a battalion.

Corpo Truppe Volontarie (CTV) Italian volunteers in Spain.

Da sbarco Amphibious Blackshirt 'M' battalions.

Fascio Bundle of fasces.

Fasci di combattimento Early Fascist organization.

Gruppo battaglioni Battalion group (containing three or four).

Guardia Nazionale Repubblicana (GNR) National Republican Guard, formed in 1943–44.

Legionario Legionnaire, unofficially used until 25 July 1943 and the official designation for the Blackshirts after Mussolini's downfall.

Legione Basic Blackshirt unit (equivalent to a regiment).

Milizia Volontaria Sicurezza Nazionale (MVSN) National Security Volunteer Militia.

Partito Fascista Repubblicano Fascist party in German-occupied Italy, 1943–45.

Raggruppamento
(pl. Raggruppamenti)   Higher echelon with two *legioni* or *gruppo battaglioni*.

Ras   Fascist local leader.

Repubblica Sociale
Italiana (RSI)   Mussolini's state in German-occupied Italy, 1943–45.

Squadra d'Azione
(pl. *Squadre d'Azione*)   Early Blackshirt organization.

Squadrista
(pl. *Squadristi*)   Member of the *Squadre d'Azione*.

Table of ranks

Blackshirt rank	Equivalent/meaning
Comandante generale	Lieutenant-general
Luogotenente generale	Major-general
Console generale	Brigadier-general
Console	Colonel
*Primo seniore**	Lieutenant-colonel
Seniore	Major
*Primo centurione**	Senior captain
Centurione	Captain
*Primo capo manipolo**	Senior lieutenant
Capo manipolo	Lieutenant
*Sotto capo manipolo**	Second lieutenant
*Primo aiutante**	Warrant officer 1st class
*Aiutante capo**	Warrant officer 2nd class
*Aiutante**	Warrant officer 3rd class
*Primo capo squadra**	Staff sergeant
Capo squadra	Sergeant
*Vice capo squadra**	Corporal
*Camicia nera scelta**	Lance corporal
Camicia nera	Private
Note	
*Rank introduced February–July 1936.	

BIBLIOGRAPHY

Unpublished sources include the *Foglio d'ordini della MVSN* (Rome, 1923–43) and documents held at the Archivio Ufficio Storico Stato Maggiore Esercito and Archivio Centrale dello Stato, both in Rome.

Acquarone, Alberto, 'La Milizia Volontaria nello stato fascista', *La Cultura*, N° 3, 1964, pp. 360–74

Battistelli, Pier Paolo, and Molinari, Andrea, *Le Forze Armate della RSI* (Milan, Hobby & Work, 2007)

Bertoldi, Silvio, *Camicia Nera* (Milan, Rizzoli, 1968)

Ferrari, Dorello, 'Il Regio Esercito e la MVSN', *Studi Storico Militari*, 1985, pp. 125–47

Galbiati, Enzo, *Il 25 luglio e la Milizia* (Milano, Bernabò, 1950)

Gatti, Luigi, *L'anima militare del fascismo – la MVSN* (PhD thesis, University of Torino, Department of History, 2003–04)

Ilari, Virgilio, and Sema, Antonio, *Marte in Orbace. Guerra, Esercito e Milizia nella Concezione Fascista della Nazione* (Ancona, Nuove Ricerche, 1988)

Jowett, Philip S., *The Italian Army 1940–45* (three volumes; Oxford, Osprey, 2000–01)

Lazzero, Ricciotti, *Il partito nazionale fascista* (Milan, Rizzoli, 1985)

Lenzi, Loris, *Dal Dnieper al Don. La 63 Legione Camicie nere Tagliamento in Russia* (Roma, Volpe, 1968)

Lucas, Ettore, and De Vecchi, Giorgio, *Storia delle unità combattenti della MVSN 1923–1943* (Rome, Volpe, 1976)

Mazzantini, Carlo, *I Balilla andarono a Salò* (Venezia, Marsilio, 1996)

Pirocchi, Angelo L., *Italian Arditi. Elite Assault Troops 1917–20* (Oxford, Osprey, 2004)

Rastrelli, Carlo, 'Un esercito in camicia nera', *Storia Militare*

Romeo di Colloredo, Pierluigi, *Emme Rossa. Le camicie nere sul fronte russo, 1941–1943* (Genova, Associazione Culturale Italia, 2008)

Rosignoli, Guido, (with the assistance of P. Crociani and L. Granata), *MVSN 1923–1943. Badges and Uniforms of the Italian Fascist Militia* (Farnham, Bird Brothers, 1980)

Rosignoli, Guido, *MVSN* (Parma, Albertelli, 1995)

Rossi, Andrea, *La Guerra delle Camicie Nere. La Milizia Fascista dalla Guerra Mondiale alla Guerra Civile* (Pisa, Franco Serantini, 2004)

Teodorani, Vanni, *Milizia Volontaria, Armata di Popolo* (Rome, CEN, 1962)

Trye, Rex, *Mussolini's Soldiers* (Airlife, 1995)

Viotti, Andrea, *Uniformi e distintivi dell'esercito italiano nella seconda guerra mondiale 1940–1945* (Rome, USSME, 1988)

INDEX